FAITH IS A VERB

FAITH IS A VERB

It Always Precedes the Miracle

a memoir by

LORRAINE FEREBEE

SHANTI ARTS PUBLISHING
BRUNSWICK, MAINE

FAITH IS A VERB

Copyright © 2022 Lorraine Ferebee
All rights reserved
No part of this book may be used or reproduced in any manner whatsoever without written permission from the publisher with the exception of brief quotations totaling one hundred or fewer words used for purposes of criticism, commentary, scholarship, or edification.

Published by Shanti Arts Publishing

Cover and interior design by Shanti Arts Designs

Cover artwork by Lynda Ozur

Shanti Arts LLC
Brunswick, Maine
www.shantiarts.com

Printed in the United States of America

Scripture quotation marked "NKJV" are taken from the New King James Version®. Copyright © 1982 by Thomas Nelson. Used by permission. All rights reserved.

Scripture quotations marked "ESV" are from the ESV® Bible (The Holy Bible, English Standard Version®), copyright © 2001 by Crossway, a publishing ministry of Good News Publishers. Used by permission. All rights reserved.

This book is a memoir, written from the author's recollections of experiences that occurred over many years. The dialogue presented in this book is not intended to represent word-for-word transcripts; events and scenes are not precise representations. The names and characteristics of some individuals have been changed to protect privacy. In all cases, the author has remained true to the feeling and meaning of what happened and what was said.

ISBN: 978-1-956056-44-0 (softcover)
ISBN: 978-1-956056-45-7 (ebook)

Library of Congress Control Number: 2022940193

Dedicated to Sally Swift

*You see then that a man is justified by works,
and not by faith only . . .
For as the body without the spirit is dead,
so faith without works is dead also.*

— James 2:24, 26 (NKJV)

CONTENTS

ACKNOWLEDGMENTS   11
PREFACE   13

THE EARLY YEARS

THE VISION   19
A PLACE WITHOUT A MAP   22
NEIGHBORHOOD FOLKS   25
GRANDMA   30
SWEET ALICE   37
THE CHURCH   44
THE GENERAL STORE   47
NAMES   50
SCHOOL   52
SAUNDRA CODE   55
FRANK OLIVER   62
JOHN ANTHONY (TONY)   65
BILL RILEY   70
ANGEL MARIA CODE   72
BOSTON TO CAPITOL HILL   75
SAUNDRA CODE CABELL   80

MORVEN PARK

THE TEST   85
DEVELOPING THE SEAT   89

SALLY SWIFT	95
THE SCHOLARSHIP	98
SECOND YEAR	100
SNAFFLES	104
CHOICES	106
GRADUATION	108

TRAINING, TEACHING, & TOURING

THE APPRENTICESHIP	133
THORNCROFT	139
SPRINGDALE FARM	142
FAMILY	146
THE ALEXANDER TECHNIQUE	148
ENGLAND	151
THORNCROFT AGAIN	153
FELKENKRAIS® SCHOOL	155
DELAWARE VALLEY COLLEGE	157
GERMANY	159

GOING HOME

VIRGINIA BEACH	165
JACKSONVILLE	169
NEW YORK	170
JACKSONVILLE AGAIN	173

ABOUT THE AUTHOR   175

ACKNOWLEDGMENTS

Grateful acknowledgments is extended to the following individuals:

Penny Smith, my Angel;
Theresa Davis, creative advisor;
Lynda Diamond, collage consultant;
Lynda Ozur, cover artist; and
Louise Meriweather and the Harlem Writer's Guild
    provided guidance and encouragement.

PREFACE

I WAS FIVE YEARS OLD AND WE WERE ON OUR WAY TO VISIT Aunt Addy in North Carolina. On the way we passed field after field of blue-green grass enclosed in four-board, white wooden fencing. This was where I saw my first horse ever. A creature of pure beauty, elegant and noble, strong and majestic, powerful yet graceful and elegant.

I saw two of them standing on their hind legs, rearing up and gently striking out at each other in a playful manner. Their spirit was so exuberant, so joy filled, something only the Creator could make. That's when I realized that they knew what they were doing, that they were thinking and planning. I became even more fascinated and determined to learn everything I could about them, especially what their needs were.

There were so many different colors among the horses we passed, and it didn't seem to matter at all. Some were standing apart, nose to tail, scratching and nuzzling each other's backs, grooming each other. Some were racing from one end of the fence line to the other. They were frolicking all about. Their eyes were so expressive and showed such sensitivity. For a few breathtaking moments, I would imagine I was riding first one of them and then the next until they passed out of sight.

I knew there was a GOD as soon as I saw the horses and I knew my destiny would include horses. My minister defines destiny as, "What God has spoken over your life." God was calling me out. It wasn't even my idea. How could a child so young become captivated, motivated, and committed for life to something? I only know one answer: I was born this way. "I have the spirit of the horse," the Ancestors would say.

I remember what it was like when we used to leave home going to visit Aunt Addy, Grandma's sister who lived an hour-and-a-half away in Sligo North Carolina. Ten years after the Emancipation Proclamation was signed in1865, the two sisters had been born on a cotton plantation in Georgia and sold together to a tobacco farmer in North Carolina. Growing up always fearing they would be sold away from each other, they insisted on their monthly visits. When we couldn't go to Aunt Addy's for any reason, or sometimes just for fun, she and her family came to our house.

The horse is a giver. He gives us his back. He allows us to sit on him, to pile our bundles and satchels on him, to carry our dead on him. He allows it. If he did not, civilization would have been sorely impacted. The fact that God made a creature whose will is to serve man in this way is astonishing to me to this day. For thousands and thousands of years humankind has nurtured and cultivated this relationship.

I want to emulate the spirit of the horse. I too want to be a giver. I have used my time with the horse to learn how to acquiesce, to soften, to listen outside the chatter in my own head, to find my true voice, to speak my truth. This journey has not been solely about horses. It has been about finding out what motivates me, over and over again, and then going for it, over and over again. Follow your path. If you don't know where you're going, ask and it will be given unto you.

This is a motivational memoir written to inspire those of you trying to find out who you are and who you want to become. You start out with only an idea, which eventually becomes a dream. The dream takes on details and becomes a passion which then blossoms into a career. If your life's work involves physical pursuits, how do you handle it when your body says no more? How does this all factor into retirement from your professional life? How much comes from your effort alone? How much is given through universal serendipity?

The first thing I learned from horses is that you can do nothing without communication. You must use your thinking, your intent, and then finally, your body to request and direct the movement of the horse. In my world, it is a request, but for many others it is a demand. They use cruel and painful methods to control the horse rather than classical training methods.

Horseback riding is character building. This is actually what I like most about it. My real purpose in teaching riding is to build strong loving character in those who seek to ride horses. Those who truly wish to learn to ride are often seeking the source of creation. By learning to be in physical harmony with another living creature, I am seeking to experience universal oneness. Therefore, to teach riding is to teach oneness. Riding is an affirmation of universal rhythm. It frees my physical and mental capacities to operate in sync with the flow of higher energies.

The most important thing I have learned is that it does not matter what you want to do with your life. You ask God first for guidance, you pray about it, you meditate on it, and when you have heard the answer, you get busy! You don't waste time wondering if you really heard anything. I've found that you don't have to know how to get there. You just have to start. The way will be made clear. Be clear about your intention and the universe will rise up to meet you wherever you are. What is God's plan for you? You don't have to know where you're going to get there. You just have to start out. You will be given the right guidance at the right time.

The equestrian life offers little paid employment for its professionals. Most come from families who have long owned and competed horses. Those growing up in that environment are competing by eight or nine years old in the US Pony Club events. Not so with me, I was actually afraid to bring up the subject at home when I was a child.

I remember what happened when I said, "I want to ride horses when I grow up" and was overheard by my grandma. "You listen here, Gal. Ain't nobody marching and going to jail for that. We're looking to move up in this world, not go round picking up manure for white folks. You should have more ambition than that! I thought I had taught you better. Don't you ever let me hear you say that again."

"Yes, Ma'am." When my grandmother spoke, "Yes, ma'am" was the only correct answer. I never mentioned it again to anyone in the family except my children years later. However, I was never any less committed to the idea and I made it my life's goal.

I was able to earn a living in a very challenging and competitive sport—the equestrian arts. Quite a story, although this is not a story about horses or equestrian arts. It is a story about faith, perseverance, and resilience. If you are curious enough to discover and exhaust new interests and seek new goals to pursue, you will continue to grow and learn. That's where I am now, wondering and open to what's next. You know, as the story line goes . . . and then what happened?

The whole point of this book is to say, you don't have to know how, you just have to know what and start out on your way. All else will be provided by your Maker.

part one

THE EARLY YEARS

THE VISION

It was dark when we left home to go to Aunt Addy's house in North Carolina. For some reason we were always very quiet getting up and dressed and into the car.

In the beginning, long before seatbelts, it was only me riding in the back seat with Grandma. She would let me have either rear window I preferred, which would depend on which side of the road the horses would be on. I even carried a used paper napkin to clean the window. Daddy Frank drove and Mama rode in the front passenger seat. As the years passed, I gained three siblings and Daddy Frank was permanently hospitalized. Now Mama always drove and Grandma took over the front passenger seat.

This left me to barter with my siblings to secure the rear window on the side of the car the horses would be on. Peppermint candy was widely used as a condiment to keep the kids quiet during the church service, and I always saved mine to barter for my rear window seat. It was a well-practiced monthly ritual. I would have my face plastered against the window pane when we arrived at Highway 17, breathlessly waiting to spot my first horse. I was going to see the horses today. To me, that meant it was going to be a very good day.

Oh, how I loved this part of the trip. These horses were not farm animals. They were sport horses being bred to compete. I would look for individual horses. There was one horse the color of a new penny I always tried to spot. I'd look for the people who took care of them to see if they looked like me. Mom would slow down as we passed to give me a longer look and Grandma never even noticed. Mama was like that. She loved a good innocent prank.

We arrived at Aunt Addy's in time to freshen up and have

breakfast before church. In the 1940s, we were still "Colored people," and there were no public accommodations for us between Virginia Beach and Sligo. Therefore, upon arrival we would form a playful line to the outhouse in the backyard and take our turn inside. Next, we would wash our face and hands on the back porch where there was a large ceramic pitcher full of fresh water and a basin with soap and face cloths.

We would then partake of a huge breakfast: ham and sausage, scrambled eggs with cheese, fried oysters, crab cakes, waffles or pancakes, fried apples and tomatoes, and huge flaky buttered biscuits, several of which I would secretly put in my purse for snacks during the long day ahead. Of course, there was coffee and tea, cold or hot, and lemonade to drink. Sunday school began at 9 a.m., followed by youth church from 11 to noon. The main service was held from noon to 2 p.m. This was followed by a hearty late lunch under the tree-canopied picnic tables behind the church. These visits were more about the two sisters seeing each other than about church. We'd have to leave for our drive back to Virginia Beach around 4:30 p.m. Highway 17 was not considered safe travel for Colored folks after dark. Leaving Aunt Addy's, I would begin my monthlong wait before I would see the horses again. This went on for ten years.

During the week we also went to church. I remember walking home from church with my grandma and a few neighbors after Wednesday night prayer meeting. Of course, I had been secretly praying for a horse. At the end of the meeting, Reverend Smith had extended "The Right Hand of God" to everyone there, his way of asking if you wanted to join the church and be baptized. I had a very strong feeling that I should go up front and stand among the initiates and prospective members. However, I was only six or seven years old and too apprehensive to go up front. I wasn't sure I knew, or they knew, what that meant. So, I didn't go. The sky was very dark that night as we walked home. Big cumulus clouds floated on the dark surface, no moon but lots of stars, and then I saw it. I saw a right hand and arm resting within the clouds. The navy-blue coat sleeve of a man wearing a white long-sleeved dress shirt with French cuffs and cufflinks that were a deep ruby red, the color of my birthstone. The fingers were extended toward me as if to shake my hand. Oh Lord. It was "The Right Hand of God." I froze. I couldn't tell my grandma because I did not want to be scolded or reprimanded again for making up stories about seeing things. But

I knew then, just as I know now, it really was "The Right Hand of God" being extended to me.

That was when I first realized there was something far more powerful than my grandma. Something that just let me know It is there. Something that showed Itself to me. At the same time, in my heart I heard the words, "I will guide your path." Somehow, in my child's mind, my secret desire to ride horses connected with the vision in the night sky and the words I had heard. In my mind, they became one because of the other. That vision became my motivator, and I would pull it up during troubling times when I felt my dream was threatened.

To this day, I can recreate the image in my mind, remembering how it felt to see that hand, how scared I was, how silent the night became as I stumbled along the barely paved road, rocks and tar, ruts and holes, unable to take my eyes off the sky. My head was tilted way back. I was hoping my grandma didn't catch on to what I was looking at. At the same time, I was hoping she would, so I'd know it was real and not my imagination. But even without her seeing it, I knew for sure what I saw and what I heard and what it meant. There have been troubling times in my life when I have recalled this vision. Each time it feels as real and reassuring as the first time.

In my teen years, I became more aware of what was going on around me. This was Virginia during the time of the Civil Rights Movement, when Dr. Martin Luther King, Jr. was leading Freedom Rides in the South. This was a time when our parents and grandparents had aspirations for us becoming professionals. They dreamed of lawyers and doctors. Clearly, Dr. King had not marched and died so that I could pay good money to learn how to "properly" pick up horse shit for white folks. Phew. That was a lot; that was heavy. I learned very quickly to keep quiet about my desire to work with horses.

I spoke it once and the look on my grandma's face let me know to never say that in her presence again. Little did she know that I did not envision myself mucking out other people's stalls, but as a skilled equestrian. Though I never mentioned it again, as the years passed, I became no less determined to follow my dream.

A PLACE WITHOUT A MAP

I GREW UP IN A PLACE THAT DIDN'T EXIST ON ANY MAP. ONLY the "Colored people" knew the name of this small community located behind a huge three-hundred-acre cornfield about three miles from the main road that connected Virginia Beach and Norfolk, Virginia. Our little neighborhood was one street, about the length of two football fields. We were a self-named section of Lynnhaven—Doyletown, just a dusty, dirt road of about fifteen houses with outdoor toilets and hand pumps in the yard for water. Our pride and joy were our vegetable gardens, so neat, clean, and well-groomed they looked like magazine pictures.

There were deep ditches on each side of the road to catch the runoff from heavy summer rains. When it rained hard for a day or more, which it often did in the summer, all the ditches would fill to overflowing, ten or twelve feet deep, especially where two ditches intersected. This would turn the neighborhood into a flood zone, which translated into a swim fest for us. "Colored people" were not allowed on Virginia Beach proper, so this was all we had in the way of an opportunity to swim. When it didn't rain, the dirt road was rutted with holes so big that if you had a car, and few did, you would often have to leave it at the beginning of the road and walk to your house. The county road grater/plow would come by every few months to smooth it out. We kids would follow the big blade of the plow, marveling at its immensity and force.

Everyone knew everyone else. We functioned as one big family, though few of us were blood related. My grandparents were the original occupants of our house. This was true for each of the families on the road. In what became the neighborhood tradition, all the houses were built by their occupants. When you were ready to build your house, you went to the lumberyard and ordered what you needed. When it was delivered, you went outside with your hammer and started making noise. This was still the custom when I was a child.

At first, there would be only the noise of one hammer. As the men walked by coming home from work, they would notice your situation and grab their hand tools and be at your side with expedience. As the new arrivals joined in the noise of pounding, sawing, and nailing, the laughing and joking would commence, growing louder and louder. The kids would join in too and be sent to fetch and carry, this and that, here and there.

The wives of these men would hurry to their kitchens as soon as they got home from work. They never consulted each other but cooked whatever they had. This time a big pan of yeast rolls usually reserved for Sunday, or biscuits. Next time maybe a banana pudding. Collard greens and cabbage would appear. Always someone with the inevitable pan of fried chicken and another of pork chops. Buckets of lemonade and sweet tea were being continuously refilled by the kids. In the summer, when the men got home around five-thirty, they could put in four or five hours before dark.

Around seven o'clock the women would arrive at the worksite with the food and everything would suddenly go completely silent. Everyone would sit about the unfinished structure or at the picnic tables or even on the ground. As the heavy-laden plates began to empty, the conversation would pick up again with the men discussing the building project and the women talking about who was sick or needed help. It was a very tight-knit and self-sustaining community. It was the job of our parents and grandparents to see to everyone else. And they did.

During the weekdays, we were maids, butlers, chauffeurs, cooks, and gardeners for the rich people who lived in town. In the late afternoons and on weekends, we were sharecroppers. We grew our own food and swapped with each other for whatever we didn't grow. No one had any money, but we lacked for nothing we knew about. So as children, we never knew we were poor. The women could all sew and made most of our clothes themselves. Lots of gathered skirts and dresses with gathered skirts were made from the beautiful gay prints of chicken feedbags. If I had "been good," I got to pick out which feedbags we brought home, ensuring which prints my dresses and skirts were made of. We were also given many hand-me-downs by the rich people we worked for, along with lots of old magazines. (So we could see pictures of what we didn't have, I sarcastically thought.)

My family grew collards, cabbage, lettuce, broccoli, corn, tomatoes, sweet and white potatoes, and strawberries. We also had grape vines and fig bushes, plus pear, apple, and peach trees. We raised and sold all manner of fowl—chickens, ducks, geese, and turkeys. We also sold their eggs. We raised and slaughtered two pigs each year. All of this we did on my grandma's eight acres of land. The neighborhood smoke house was in my grandma's backyard, so there was always something going on at home. There were no lights outside at night anywhere, except for the moon and the lightening bugs, which we captured and put in mason jars for our amusement. We always let them go before they died.

At winter's end, all thoughts turned to planting. The neighborhood elders would have a meeting, usually on my grandma's front porch, to decide who planted what. By the end of the meeting, each family knew what and how much they were to plant and harvest in order to have enough for their family and enough to barter with the neighbors for whatever they did not grow themselves. There were no hungry people in my neighborhood, just a wonderful cast of unique characters.

NEIGHBORHOOD FOLKS

There was Miss Captola Tucker, who we called MamaCap. She grew the most beautiful flowers you'd ever see. Her yard was a botanical garden and arboretum all rolled into one. She taught us the names of the plants and made games of spelling the names correctly. There was always something blooming in her yard. She tended her plants early every morning before the sun was up and again late in the afternoon just before the sun went down. She would be pruning and weeding and watering every day except Sunday. She was a large, tall woman in a long dress wearing a freshly ironed apron with a pocket on the right thigh, which contained her handkerchief. She always wore a big straw hat and a big smile and always had time to stop and chat, even with us children. MamaCap sold penny candy and was always surrounded by children, which was why she sold penny candy. If you didn't have a penny, she'd give you the candy anyway. All the kids wanted to help her in her garden because she paid us for our work with penny candy. With several of her neighbors' children in tow, MamaCap could be easily found working among her flowers, which she also regarded as her children.

MamaCap had a granddaughter, Estelle. She and I went to Norfolk every Saturday morning to take piano lessons. I was determined not to learn to play the piano because I knew that if I did, I would have to play in church every Sunday. So most of the time we spent the money at the donut shop. I practiced the same song for over a year before Grandma let me quit. I always thought it was so amazing that such poor people found a way to provide pianos and musical instruments. They felt it was so important for us kids to learn music.

Miss Cherry Sawyer and her sister, Miss Edna, lived next door to MamaCap. Miss Cherry loved cats, and her backyard and porch always had an assortment of colorful well-fed cats lounging about under the shade trees next to the back porch. The porch was screened in and contained her private collection of unusually beautiful cats. She had been known to give away a few of the cats lounging under the trees, but those on the back porch were hers for keeps. Whenever we ate seafood for dinner, I was always sent to take the scraps to Miss Cherry for her cats. The two sisters both went to our church. Miss Edna was quiet and had a funny-sounding gravelly voice. Miss Cherry sang in the senior choir. She did not have a pleasant singing voice, but that did not diminish her enthusiasm or volume. She had the most off-key and the loudest voice in the choir except for my grandma's. Miss Edna was also an usher at church and lived to be over 100 years old.

Miss Bell Sevills, who like her daughter, Irma, weighed over 250 pounds, lived across the road from Miss Cherry and Miss Edna. They did not go to church and were rarely seen, as they were too large to move about freely. They seemed to spend their lives sitting on the front porch, watching the goings-on in the neighborhood. They were my grandma's best source of information if she needed to know who went where and did what. We had "neighborhood watch" in the 1950s on our little country road.

Uncle and Auntie, Ananias and Ellen Ferebee, lived directly across the road from our house. Though they had the same last name as my grandma, we were not blood related. They had no children of their own and were called Uncle and Auntie by everyone, children and adults alike. They gave every child in the neighborhood something for Christmas, usually socks or underwear. Uncle was the chauffeur and Auntie was the maid for the Bingham family, who were big landowners in town. The Binghams bought a new car every two years and gave Uncle and Auntie the one they replaced. Therefore, every two years Uncle and Auntie had a new two-year-old car. But since no one had ever driven the car except Uncle, I always wondered if he realized it had always been his car from the beginning. Uncle was the superintendent of Sunday school and a deacon as well. Girls were warned not to be alone with him. Auntie was an usher, and they never missed a Sunday at church. Their yard was surrounded by the neatest, greenest, four-foot-high box hedge in the neighborhood. They were the first in the neighborhood to get a TV and proudly placed it face-out toward the yard. Every Saturday afternoon the kids would gather sitting cross-legged on the lawn in front of the porch to watch cowboy movies, which I loved because cowboys rode horses. Protected behind the hedge from the passersby, road noise, and dust, Auntie would serve us all popcorn and sodas. It was a kind of open-air theatre.

Clarice and Margie Harper lived next door to us. Their dad had a civil service job and sent them to Catholic school in Norfolk. They were the rich folks in our community and the envy of every girl in the neighborhood because of their beautiful store-bought clothes. Miss LillieMae, their mom, spared no expense on their attire. She was also a maid, but better paid than most. She worked for only the wealthiest families down on the south end of the beach. Even though both Clarice and Margie wore uniforms to school, they still got new clothes every September when school started. I looked forward to them getting new clothes because they always cleaned out their closet and gave me their last year's now old clothes, which became my this year's new clothes. They actually had clothes closets built in along their bedroom walls, something their Dad had copied from a magazine.

They gave me many wool-pleated skirts with blouses and sweaters to match, along with shoes and boots for each outfit. Though they wore size eight and nine and my feet were size ten or eleven, I wore them anyway. You can actually train yourself to walk as though your feet don't hurt even though they are killing you. I still carry the evidence of that on my feet today. Clarice and Margie went to the Baptist Church with us sometimes and even sang in the teen choir. They didn't go to Catholic school for religious reasons but because the education was thought to be superior there, and they were planning on attending college. Unlike the rest of us, their dad could afford it. He had a good gov'ment job.

Their grandmother, Miss Lucy Harper, lived on the other side of them and did not work. She had the only telephone in the neighborhood. It was a party line, which meant you could hear other people's conversations if someone was already using the line when you tried to make a call. There was usually a line of people waiting on her porch to use the telephone. Miss Lucy would serve you lemonade and potato chips while you waited your turn. We loved Miss Lucy but thought it a bit odd that she did not go to church yet seemed perfectly kind and thoughtful just the same. Hmm!

Mr. Hawkins and Miss Maddie lived at the end of the road. They both drank a lot and were usually yelling at each other about nothing in particular. Mr. Hawkins and his mule plowed everybody's garden and all the planting fields in the neighborhood without charge in exchange for food at harvest time. It was a beautiful sight when everybody's garden was being tilled and plowed at the same time. The smell of fresh earth would permeate the air. It was a celebratory time. His mule was old and ill-kept and sometimes had a mind of his own. He would simply refuse to move at all, no matter the insult or abuse heaped upon him. Whatever you had planned to do would have to wait another day. He looked tired and was not well-fed, his ribs clearly visible, and grooming was completely foreign to him. I worked out a deal with Mr. Hawkins. I was to keep him supplied with iced tea or lemonade and the mule supplied with fresh water the whole time they were plowing. In return, I could sit on the mule when they plowed the last row. The mule didn't even seem to notice I was there. This mule did not at all resemble the horses I saw on Route 17. As a small child, I didn't even know they were related. The mule was a lowly farm animal. The horses I saw on our trips were well-fed sport horses raised to compete in equestrian sports. I felt sorry for the mule. I saw him as a slave. The sport horses I saw as Olympic athletes.

In my teen years, I made my grandma's life miserable on purpose. In my struggle for independence, it seemed to me that anything I wanted to do, she was against. So I decided to do to her what I thought she was doing to me—stand in the way of anything she wanted or stood for. I would deliberately do just the opposite of what she wanted. With enthusiasm, I would defy her at every opportunity. Since Clarice and Margie went to Catholic school, they also sometimes went to Catholic Church in the city. I decided to become Catholic so that I could go to the city with them on Sundays. No more singing in the choir, leading prayer, or delivering welcome addresses and responses. No Women's Day paper, no Negro History recitation, no Christmas play. Wow! How can she object? Even she says that God is everywhere. Why can't I talk to him at St. Vincent's? We know how well this went over with Grandma. However, she did allow me to continue going to midnight Mass on Christmas Eve.

I had three best friends: Estelle, Barbara, and Virginia. Estelle was MamaCap's granddaughter and lived closest to my house. I saw her most often. Barbara and her parents lived at the end of the road. Virginia lived halfway between Estelle and Barbara. She lived with her aunt who was my mom's drinking buddy. In the summer we spent most of each day walking back and forth from one of our houses to the other. The conversations, the jokes, the tears, the hurts, the lies we told were endless, as boundless as our imaginations. Lots of slow, lazy, summertime walking, often in the blazing sun, with hysterical laughter about nothing at all. We grew up together on that road from the time we were girls of four and five years old and became the old women with gray hair who have lunch together whenever I'm in Virginia Beach. We have gone to the funerals of our children together. We brag about our children, grandchildren, and now even our great-grandchildren.

Boobie and Miss Sarah lived on the other side of our house. Boobie washed his car and enjoyed his drink on Saturdays. I loved for him to wash his car because he always played the radio real loud. It was my only chance to hear jazz and pop music. Grandma did not allow that kind of music, the devil's music, in our house. The more whiskey he drank, the louder the music got. I was rooting for Boobie, "Drink, Boobie, drink"! Miss Sarah baked the best yeast rolls in the neighborhood and was heavily relied upon for wedding receptions and funeral repasts. The neighborhood was teeming with talent.

GRANDMA

My early years were spent with my grandma, Miss Angerona to all who knew her personally and Miss Ferebee to those who did not. We all lived with Grandma: my mother and stepdad, Daddy Frank; and my siblings, Joseph, Gloria, and Benjamin (or Junior as he was called in the neighborhood to distinguish him from his father who was also named Benjamin).

In one of my earliest memories, I'm tilling soil with my hands, letting it run through my fingers. My grandma is telling me how rich and beautiful our soil is. She tells me it has taken her many years of feeding the soil for it to become so rich. We're preparing a flowerbed for seeding in the front yard when she tells me to "smell the soil and then taste it." I thought tasting the soil was a strange thing for her to ask me to do.

It tastes surprisingly good, rich and warm and a little pungent. "This is how your soil should taste before you put your seeds in. Now add a little water," she said, "not enough to make it wet, just moist. Wouldn't you like to be the seed that gets covered in this wonderful smell and feel? Then when the sun comes out, you'd break ground and feel sunlight for the first time. You'd open your petals and break free just because you'd be so warm and cozy you'd feel like going out to play." She made it an inspiring story. I wanted to be that seed by the time she was finished.

"What color would you want to be if you were a flower?" she asked.

"A beautiful blue-green with a touch of yellow," I answered.

"Me too," she said.

I was so happy because I thought that meant we both wanted to be alike. It was wonderful to watch her handle the soil. She did it with such reverence and respect. It reminded me of the way she handled the Bible, with respect for its sacredness. She had a relationship with the soil and didn't mind eating a little dirt to get what she wanted. This became a life lesson for me.

She taught me how to "kick-ass" with just my eyes. She would be appalled to hear herself described with such foul language. She never used curse words or foul language. I don't remember ever hearing her raise her voice to anyone or speak unkindly about anyone, at least not in front of them. She didn't have to. She was the law of the land. The neighbors, merchants, church folks, even the sheriff, all thought my grandma was in charge of everything, and so did she. She never spoke a cuss word, just leveled a cold, hard, penetrating stare that could travel around corners and that you could physically feel. She was the glue that held everything together, not just for our household, but the whole neighborhood.

I went everywhere she went, whether I wanted to or not. I was like her shadow, constantly at her side, visiting the sick and shut-in, taking the train to town to sell vegetables when we or the neighbors had excess produce, and to church—always to church.

My grandma owned our house and eight acres. My grandfather and four of their six sons, along with the neighbors, had built the house. The mortgage had been paid off by my uncles who had all moved north in search of better paying jobs, so we were no longer sharecroppers. By the time I was born, Grandpa Charlie had passed away.

The house was spotless inside its five downstairs rooms with an unfinished attic upstairs. Grandma slept in the front bedroom, opposite the living room on the front of the house. Her room was like a sentry post. She controlled the front door from that room. I can remember having to sleep with her in her bed when we had overnight guests and my room was needed for them. It was hard to act as though I didn't hear or smell anything when she passed gas, which she did a lot. She never detected either my gagging or my sniggles.

Grandma lived in the kitchen, the vegetable and flower gardens, at the quilting frame, and of course at church, which took up by far the majority of her time. The kitchen was small, well-organized, immaculate, and efficient. The old wood-burning stove had five eyes on top and a very large oven for baking and roasting meat. There was a bread-warming compartment above.

Four nights a week from seven to nine o'clock, any of the neighborhood women who wanted to earn money were invited to my grandma's dining room to quilt. When she sold the quilts, she was very generous with those who had worked. The amount each person received reflected how many hours they had worked, and everybody kept close track of everyone else's hours. It was sort of a game played for bragging rights.

The quilts sold for $300 to $500 each. A patron could choose fabric, color, and pattern. They would be given a delivery date and pay a deposit of one-half the cost so Grandma could purchase what she needed to do the job. They would come back in two or three weeks to pick up the finished product. Her quilts were very expensive and that's how she wanted them. These ladies completed at least two quilts each month.

Some of the quilters cut out the squares and others pieced them together. They were then sewn into strips of cloth to form rows. The rows were sewn together by another group. There would be three or four work groups in the room, sort of an assembly line. This was the basic process for all the quilts. It was only the size, pattern, and fabric that varied. Everything from women's stockings formed into delicate rosettes, to linen and silk were used. Even old wool coats were cut up and made into squares. Cotton was the hands-down favorite fabric because it was easy to wash. Quilts made from old coats were my favorite to sleep under on a cold winter night. They were so heavy they'd keep you warm just from their weight alone. You were considered blessed if you had one, and I did and I still do.

Grandma was an entrepreneur. Although I doubt she ever heard that word, certainly not in reference to herself. She made, sold, and traded medicines, quilts, clothes, and jams and jellies from the fruit of her own apple, peach, pear, and fig trees.

She also took in laundry from the wealthy white people who lived in town—the same folks who ordered and bought the quilts. Grandma might have taken in the laundry, but it was my little sister, Gloria, and I who did the actual washing and ironing. We had to achieve perfection with no "cat faces," which is what she called wrinkles. These were the shirts of the doctors, lawyers, bankers, and city council members. This connection meant she could and did avail herself of their services, without charge, when needed. So, no mistakes were allowed.

In order to get hot water for washing clothes, cooking, bathing, and life in general, we started by dragging dead branches and small limbs from the woods beyond our corn field to our yard—the job of my brothers, Ben and Joe. Hurricane season always ensured we'd have plenty to choose from. The boys would cut them into one-foot lengths, which would fit not only the pot-bellied stove in the dining room that heated the whole house but also the kitchen cookstove. My sister and I would pick up twigs and split the smaller pieces into even smaller pieces of wood to create kindling for fire starters.

Gloria and I would take turns pumping water on the hand pump in the backyard and carrying it by bucket to the large, galvanized tub out by the clothesline on the other side of the house. The big old tub was the same one we took our baths in. The tub was set on three stacks of three bricks, evenly spaced. We made a fire under the tub to heat the water. Then we would pump more water to cool the heated water to the temperature dictated by Grandma. It was my job to wash or scrub, if need be, the clothes on the washing board. I preferred the glass to the metal washboard. The glass one did not tear up the clothes when the fabric was delicate.

More water had to be pumped to fill the two rinse tubs. The second rinse contained the bluing that was used to keep the white clothes from yellowing. Finally, we would hang the laundry on the clotheslines strung between two oak trees. We also kept two buckets of fresh water in the kitchen for drinking. Those buckets were never less than half-full of clean, fresh water. The result of forgetting this responsibility was unforgettably painful. Somebody was getting chastised and the switch would be applied. Pumping water was constant, as were other assigned chores like cutting wood. We used a lot of water, so we pumped a lot of water. If we didn't get enough rain, we also had to water all of the plants we grew in the gardens and fields if we were going to eat.

Electricity came to Doyletown when I was five or six years old and with it the electric iron, refrigerator, and radio. Oh boy! What fun we had sitting around the dining room table listening to *Amos 'n' Andy* on the radio. It came on right after homework. I still wonder why we sat around the table to listen to the radio.

At first Grandma wouldn't allow my mom to put the new electric refrigerator in the kitchen. It was placed on the back porch with the electric cord running through the window, a clear fire hazard. Grandma said, "I'm not going to put my food in no electric box and let that stuff get into my system." After a few weeks, she relented, and the refrigerator and its cord were finally put in the kitchen. Her icebox, which she continued to use for her food, was placed on the back porch.

The wringer washer was another matter. It attacked Grandma one day, catching her arm in the rollers. We were able to stop the rollers before she was actually injured but she would never touch the thing again. Before electricity, we would iron clothes in the kitchen because that's where we heated the iron, made of actual iron, on the wood-burning stove. Now we could iron in any room where there was an outlet, and you could preset the temperature.

Wildflowers decorated the landscape and medicinal herbs grew abundantly. There were birds galore and bird calls to identify. My mother and the other night crew workers who took the last bus home at midnight never took the path through the woods. Even though it added another fifteen minutes to their walk, they stayed on the road. White folks had been known to ambush us on that path at night.

Grandma made potions and salves from the plants and roots found in these woods. Her advice was well regarded and sought after by many in the neighborhood. Whenever someone was not feeling well or had a slight injury, they'd visit or send for my grandma. Usually, they'd get a jar or paper bag containing something she'd made from a plant or root I'd been sent to gather from the woods. She would give me a basket of cuttings, plants she wanted me to find and bring back. Her instructions were, "Don't come back until you find some of each and every one." Often, depending on the season, weather, and my diligence, or lack thereof, this could take all day. YEAH! HOORAY!

Grandma was, and is still, the most influential person I've ever known. Her strength, perseverance, and leadership set her apart. Her faith, love, and support were demonstrated time and time again. She taught me and the entire neighborhood the one lesson she wanted to instill in us all: "Once you decide on something you want to do or accomplish, with God's blessing just keep putting one foot in front of the other and your needs will be provided. You'll get there. Don't ever give up. You can do it, no matter what it is." That was her message. Regardless of the situation or circumstances, her message remained the same.

When I was four years old, my mom married my stepdad, Daddy Frank. My biological dad had married the woman he was engaged to when he met my mother. Daddy Frank was an exterior painter for the Norfolk Naval Base. One day he fell from a ladder on the eighth floor to the ground. Although he recovered physically, his head injuries were severe, and he was sent away to the state mental hospital where he died a few years later. Before this accident our family had grown to include my brother Ben, four years my junior and with whom I shared a birthday; my sister, Gloria, six years my junior; and my brother Joseph, eight years younger. My mother was now left alone with four children and an elderly mother to support.

My mother's bedroom was on the same side of the house as Grandma's, in between Grandma's bedroom and the kitchen, which was on the back of the house. It was impossible to enter or exit Mom's room without Grandma knowing about it.

All of us kids slept in the attic. The steps were in the kitchen.

When you first got to the top of the stairs, there was a china closet to your immediate right. It had glass panes in front up top, and it locked. The doors on the bottom also locked. It was used to form a wall and behind it were my grandma's quilting supplies, piles and piles of neatly folded, color-coordinated cloth pressed and laid out, waiting to be chosen to go into a quilt. The old china closet was full of old college textbooks that belonged to my Uncle Lewis. I could see the books through the glass panes and had read the titles so many times I could recite them by heart. My grandma kept the keys, so there was no chance I was going to get to read one of them, even though he had graduated from college many years ago. At that time, he was the only member of our family to have graduated from college. Those books were next to sacred—forbidden territory—and my grandma revered them above all other books except the Bible.

I was eight or nine years old when I first pried away the back of the old china closet. If I was very careful, I could take the back off the cabinet and remove any book I wished. That's how I discovered the Greek myths. OMG! My imagination soared. That's when I began to travel, to go places that existed only in my imagination, to know that other worlds really could and did exist. I never got caught stealing books from the china closet, but it did cement my reading habit. No longer was I satisfied with coloring books and light reading when waiting for my mom and dad while they had their secret rendezvous. I started demanding real books with real stories, sometimes even about horses.

My sister and I slept in the middle room that had double windows at each end and was about thirty feet long. We thought we were really blessed because the brick chimney from the wood stove downstairs ran through our room. Unlike most everyone else in the house, we kept warm and toasty all winter long.

My two brothers slept in the front bedroom facing the road and had to pass through our room to get to theirs. Therefore, my sister and I had to stay covered from head to toe whenever we were in bed for fear my brothers would see our private parts. Even today as a late senior citizen, I am unable to be comfortable in bed unless I'm completely covered from my neck to my feet no matter the weather.

My family believed in hard work and prayer, and yes, in that order. That is why "A person is justified by works and not by faith alone." (James 2:24, ESV) You have to do something FIRST. "If you really believe it, act on it now," Grandma would say.

My mother worked two jobs and sometimes three. She did day work for five dollars a day, plus one dollar for bus fare. She also worked at Snow White Laundry five nights a week to earn another forty-five dollars. Men's dress shirts were her specialty. She pressed shirts from 5 p.m. until midnight for many years, taking the last bus home, and walking the last two miles at 12:30 in the morning.

Sometimes in the summer, when school was out and I could get a ride with a neighbor or had bus fare, I'd meet my mom at the laundry at 5 p.m. and work her shift for her so she could have a break. She'd sneak off, go to the bootlegger's house for a few minutes, and then sit with me, telling stories of where she had been or still wanted to go. Many of our neighbors worked the night shift at the laundry and at hotels on the beach. They all took the last bus home too.

They made a jolly walk of that trip, laughing and joking those last two miles, knowing the tales would be repeated and enlarged the next night. When it was raining, those two miles seemed like forever. That was my mom's life, year after year. She struggled to provide food, clothes, education, gas, electricity, transportation, and everything in between.

Mom worked hard during the week and played hard on the weekends. The weekends were her only chance to have a life, to be Sweet Alice, to find some relief from the grind, to laugh, play, and enjoy life as best she could because Monday through Friday she was in bondage for the rest of her life. You'd never know all that, though, because she was forever playing tricks and making merry, with the help of a little vodka.

I learned humility and compassion from my mother. Find a way to be YOU. Find a way to enjoy your life and have fun. Yes, do your job, fulfill your responsibilities and obligations, but don't let it sour your personality and strip you of your joy or your goals. Create a life for yourself, one that includes no one but you. Don't settle for slavery again in another form.

I learned discipline, punctuality, dependability, and a work ethic from both my mother and my grandmother. They were both "all about it." I can still hear my grandma say, "Colored folks got enough going against them already. You don't need to add being late to the list. You must always be prompt, clean and well-groomed, well-dressed and well-spoken. Your references must be impeccable, and you must arrive at least five minutes early for any appointment you have anywhere, for the rest of your life." I still am today. Between the two of them and help from the church and neighbors, we had everything we needed.

SWEET ALICE MEETS BOOKER T

ALICE THELMA NAOMI FEREBEE WAS HER LEGAL NAME. Sweet Alice, that's how I thought of my mother. She really was a sweet and loving person. She was also beautiful and refined. There was a gentleness, a softness about her. She carried herself with poise and dressed with a flattering grace. Her voice was soft and sultry. She wore a constant happy smile and brought an upbeat, playful energy, no matter how tired she was. She was nurturing and protective. Oh, to have her hold my hand or put her arm around my waist as we walked together was enough for me to be content and happy. My mother taught me kindness and compassion.

Her big break, so she thought at that time, came when she was thirty-three years old and was asked to go north for a summer to Bethesda, Maryland, just outside of Washington, DC, as the maid and babysitter for the Pruitts, one of the wealthy families she did "day work" for on Virginia Beach. She had always been under her mother's strict supervision until this point. Saturday was her day off, and in her wanderings, she stumbled upon the Howard University campus and library. She had never imagined a library could be this big, with so many books on so many subjects. She began to spend all her Saturdays there. The place smelled of old books and she found it totally enchanting. There was no place like this at home. She had never seen so many books about Negroes and was determined to read them all no matter how long it took. Though the school library was open to the public, checking out books was not allowed unless you were affiliated with the University. Mom saw to it that she and the librarian became friendly very quickly. This allowed her to privately check out one book each week. What a privilege! She was awestruck and became an avid and insatiable reader.

It was there in 1942 that she met my father, Booker T. Powell. He also spent Saturdays in the library, cramming to ensure that he remained the academic leader of his class. When the two met, it was love at first sight for my mom. Being away from home and my grandma's prying eyes didn't hurt. For my dad, it was pure lust with a little boost of confidence from the bourbon he had hidden in his pocket. Together they produced my mother's shame: a very strong willed, opinionated, daughter, and therefore I AM.

After a couple months of making small talk, he invited her to the drugstore for a soda. Then a few weeks later he invited her to a bar for a beer. A few weeks more and he invited her to his dorm room for a drink—bourbon. She had never experienced any of this before and was overwhelmed and thrilled with all the attention. The few young men brave enough to try to date were unable to withstand my grandmother's scrutiny. This time she was in love. He told her she was beautiful and began to introduce her to things about her body she had never known. She was very excited by all this attention and eager to learn more. She could hardly wait until her next day off.

It was excruciatingly painful when the Pruitts returned to their Virginia Beach residence in the winter and she was unable to see Booker T. Mom even kept the letters they wrote to each other during those times and shared them with me all those many years later. Once back in Virginia Beach, Mom would wait eagerly through the winter until she and the Pruitts returned once again to Bethesda for the summer.

It was on such an occasion and after too much bourbon that she didn't stop him this time when he began to teach her one more new thing about her body. Though briefly painful, she grew to enjoy this new way of sharing. Her naiveté notwithstanding, that's what he told her it was. It was so exciting, partly because it defied her mother's admonitions. She felt like an adult for the first time. In DC, she was a true grown-up and could do whatever she wanted.

It was less than a year after they met that Mom had to break the news to her mother, my grandma. She had to tell her she was pregnant and that my father wouldn't marry her. Though he always maintained he loved her, she was only a maid and he was about to graduate from Howard University. As the first college graduate in his tribe, he had to marry someone befitting his station in life. He was the son of a Lumbee Indian and a high yaller Negro woman, the daughter of a white slave master who had run away from the plantation and ended up on the coast of North Carolina along the Lumbee River.

It was Booker T's responsibility and duty to bring prestige and honor to his father. No one else in their tribe had ever gone to college, and the whole Lumbee Nation was invested in his future, which included his choice of a wife. She had to be a college graduate and my mother didn't qualify. He had to marry up. He had already met and proposed to the lucky lady before he met my mother. She, too, was a student at Howard University and had already said yes to Booker T's proposal of marriage. All this just slipped his mind for a few months. His wife-to-be came from a very well-to-do Negro family that had grown to prominence through the slave trade. This was thought to bring additional financial security to the Lumbee Nation. His father approved. My mom couldn't compete. She had no dowry and no college degree.

Because she held such a position of leadership in the community and the church, my grandma's worst fear was that her daughter would be an unwed mother. Sweet Alice was sent to Aunt Addy's in North Carolina until the baby was born. In that way, no one would know what a disgrace my mom had become. The neighbors would think she was in Bethesda with the Pruitts as usual. My grandma was to go visit Aunt Addy when the time came for my mom to deliver and mysteriously adopt a baby. My mom would remain at Aunt Addy's for another month to recover. So when my mom came back from pretending to be in Bethesda, she would be greeted at home by my grandma and a new little sister—me. My mother went immediately back to work, while my grandma became my mother and took on the task of raising me.

This farce went on until my father started demanding to see me because he was sending my mother money to provide for me. He wasn't allowed on Grandma's property because he had "ruint" my mother's reputation and thereby hers. My dad's nickname was Flat Top, for the obvious reason that his head had a flat top. Through the grapevine, he had heard that I looked just like him, flat top included, and he wanted to claim his bragging rights since he was paying good money. Grandma finally relented and allowed him to come onto "her" property, so it had become clear to the whole neighborhood that Booker T was my dad. So began the monthly visits. Grandma even started allowing him to bring my Christmas and birthday presents to our house instead of leaving them across the road with the neighbors.

On the second Saturday of each month, my mother would wake me up early and get me freshly bathed, combed, and dressed for Dad's arrival. I'd sit out on the front porch watching the end of the road with great anticipation for his car to appear. It was a big black Lincoln with whitewall tires. It made me feel so important because all the neighbors would be watching. He was always late, exiting the car with a big laugh, exclaiming, "Procrastination is the thief of time, Flat Top." We'd go for a ride in his car if he hadn't already had too much to drink. If he had, we would sit on a neighbor's porch and chitchat. If he had been drinking, it wouldn't be wise to sit on my grandma's porch. He had the Native American problem with alcohol.

When we went for a ride, it was most often to Norfolk where my father would hang out in the auto repair shop with his friends for a while. Then we'd go visit Miss Jenny, where he was usually joined by my mother. They had to travel separately and secretly in order to keep my grandma from finding out they were still seeing each other, in spite of the fact that he would not marry her and was now married to someone else. Even though my dad married Miss Ruby when he graduated from college, he and my mother never actually stopped seeing each other. My mom and Miss Jenny were also friends. Miss Jenny's house was a "party" house and Mom sometimes went to visit her alone. She always had candy and coloring books, and I was allowed to play with her collection of beautiful dolls from all over the world. Miss Jenny was a bootlegger. She sold liquor by the bottle or the shot. She also rented rooms. After a few shots of vodka for my mom and bourbon for my dad, the two of them would disappear for a while. I would be left with my new books under the watchful eye of Miss Jenny. Her customers would come and go, some couples disappearing into back rooms or upstairs for a while and then happily reappearing. Miss Jenny also cooked and served dinners. A good time was had by all, especially me—I thought.

After Dad got married, we didn't hang out at Miss Jenny's as often for a while. Whenever he came to visit, we would go to the auto repair shop where he and his cronies hung out. I didn't think it was really an auto repair shop because I never saw anyone working on anything except whatever bottle was almost empty. After a few minutes of bragging about his beautiful smart daughter, he'd have a few more drinks and forget I was even there. So once again, I would be left sitting on the bench in front of the auto repair shop to inspect and conjecture about the city folks and how they behaved. Once I even saw a drunk woman! I would sit there and be entertained by all the passersby. I loved it! He'd always have lots of new books or paper dolls to keep me occupied, but I much preferred to people watch. I still do today.

The city people were very different from the people in my rural neighborhood. Everybody talked very loud and swore a lot. They wore their church clothes every day of the week. Even when their clothes were dirty and ragged, they were still fancy by my standards, high styled and in bright colors, what my grandma would call loud colors.

After it got dark in the summer, around nine o'clock, I'd start to worry about having an automobile accident on the way home because Dad was always pretty drunk by that time. So I'd ride the twenty miles home from Norfolk to Virginia Beach with my eyes closed, mostly holding my breath, and praying silently as we swerved back and forth across Route 58.

My father's new wife, Miss Ruby, would not allow me to come into "her" house through the front door, although it was my father's money that paid for the house. I had a hard time trying to understand this and why Dad seemed to have no say in the matter. The first time I met her, I decided she was really ugly, not because of how she looked but because of what she said. "Booker T, don't you ever bring 'her' through my front door again. Take her round back where you keep the dogs since she came from your bitch." I didn't know what she meant. Was she calling my mother a female dog? I had already learned that I was a bastard inasmuch as I was born out of wedlock, but now I learned that I was a bastard born of a bitch. Since he made no reply, hung his head, and took me 'round back like she said, I thought maybe she was right. I was tormented for months trying to understand what she had meant. After that, we never went to his house again, and our regular visits to Miss Jenny's party house resumed. He did try to excuse her behavior by explaining that she could not have children and couldn't bring herself to accept me because of that.

Many years later I learned she had disgraced my dad. Yes, she was a college graduate, and her family once had lots of money, land, and slaves. Not only could she not have children, she was also widely known to be a bull dagger as well. She was also co-owner of a much-publicized jazz club in Norfolk. In those days, when we were called Negroes, in my neighborhood lesbians were called bull daggers.

With Daddy Frank institutionalized and Miss Ruby living the high life, back to Miss Jenny's we went when Dad and Mom wanted to see each other. If it was just going to be Dad and me, we went to Virginia Beach. He'd usually drop me off at the hairdresser for two or three hours. It was always bittersweet. I loved getting my hair done and how beautiful I felt when Miss Wilson was finished. I couldn't wait to get my first look in the mirror. But I hated the way my dad would smell when he returned to pick me up. He smelled like sour milk or rancid food. I still get nauseous if I smell bourbon. He'd walk unsteadily, sometimes he even missed a step or two altogether, and his language would have changed. He'd say a lot of bad words, which he usually did not do. Time to start praying again, praying that we get home in one piece. But then again, this might be a good time to get a pair of new shoes out of him since he clearly doesn't know what he's doing. Maybe we should go to the shopping plaza so he can use his credit cards... but then someone I know might see him stumbling about. Okay, back to praying...

When he died in 1965, my mother insisted I go to his funeral. I didn't want to go, but Mom had my younger brother, Joseph, escort my two sons and me. Miss Ruby, my dad's wife was still glaring at me some forty-five years later. No one knew who I was, but they all kept commenting on "how much that woman and the two little boys look just like Booker T, all three 'Flat Tops.'" For my part, I was shocked to see a roomful of people who looked just like me. I froze. Instead of going forth to meet them and taking advantage of the moment, I was shocked into silence. My heart was beating so fast I almost ran from the place. I couldn't get out of there fast enough. I simply did not know what to say to a room full of Lumbee Indians.

I realized then that I had never really known him at all. I had never had a conversation with him about anything that I can remember, except when I became pregnant. He was never affectionate and never showed any physical expression of love or caring. Yet he continued to come and visit. He was still there when my two sons were born and took them on the same Saturday morning outings that he once took me. He'd pick up his two "little Flat Tops" and off they'd go. I can't say I knew him, but I did love him. Still left on my bucket list is a trip to Lumberton, North Carolina, the home of the Lumbee Nation.

THE CHURCH

On Sunday we prayed for everyone and everything imaginable. We collected money for the sick and the shut-ins. We delivered plates of food to their homes from the picnic tables and repast after church. We had Christmas and Easter plays, and special celebrations and occasions that required us to spend a lot of time in rehearsals practicing our performances.

The church was the backbone of the neighborhood. If you wanted to find someone, you went to the church because even if that person was not there, someone would know where to look. Lynnhaven Baptist Church was a wonderful, supportive, loving, hopeful community. Sunday school began at 9 a.m. I, per Grandma's orders of course, was a Sunday school teacher by the age of nine. There was a little candy store next door to the church, and all the kids would run to the store after Sunday school to get a snack or soda pop before the main service began. Usually, if you had a quarter, you'd have enough change left for the collection plate. If you didn't have any money, you probably had a biscuit or buttered roll in your pocket.

The first time I addressed the congregation I was five years old. I was so small I had to stand on a wooden box behind the minister's podium to be seen. By the time I was twelve years old, I vowed that when I became a grown-up, I was not going to church. I reasoned that after going to church five or six times a week for my whole life, I had already gone to church enough for one lifetime.

The main Sunday service ran from noon to 3 p.m. and was all about fire and brimstone and the building fund. Miss Patience Malby would get touched by the Holy Spirit and "get happy" and begin running up and down the center aisle with arms flailing, shouting and praising God, especially when she was wearing a new dress. The preacher would be doing a lot of hollering about the wages of sin. You were supposed to learn to fear God and be too scared to sin. It didn't work for me. I liked to sit with Mama who would usually be showing me some lady's hat that needed to have its flowers watered. Did you know that laughing until you cry, until you pee in your pants, without making one sound, can be masked as overcome by the Holy Spirit? Mama and I got "happy" almost every time we sat together.

When I could not sit with Mom, I had to sit with the other children who occupied the first two or three pews. There we could be easily observed by everyone, including the pastor and the choir, of which my grandmother was a member. We would have to sit there absolutely quiet and still and appear to give our undivided attention to the preacher. Any misbehavior or inattentiveness was dealt with rather harshly: Immediately after the service, you'd be taken out behind the church and sent into the woods to fetch a switch to the liking of the switcher. The worst part of this experience was not the pain from the switch but making sure you did not holler loud enough to be heard around the front of the church by your peers—totally embarrassing.

After the service ended, around 3 p.m., there was a repast under the canopied shade trees. Each family would unveil their picnic basket filled with goodies and share with everyone else. There were always lots of comparisons about who made the best fried chicken or sweet potato pie with everyone vying to get some from whoever was deemed to have the "best." Buckets of lemonade and sweet tea were consumed, along with the best yeast rolls you ever had. They'd usually still be warm from the oven and dripping with butter. After the repast was BYPU, Baptist Young People's Union, from 5 to 7 p.m. It was mostly more prayer and congregational singing, poem recitations, and at holiday times, rehearsals for the Christmas or Easter plays. From 7 to 8 p.m., there was prayer meeting and testimony in the main sanctuary.

Evening service began at 8 and was over around 10 p.m. By this time, all of us kids would be so tired we'd usually be fighting sleep. This could mean another switching, so you tried hard to stay awake and ready to nudge your neighbors if they started to nod off. There was also prayer meeting on Wednesday night and choir practice every Friday night. There were five choirs: children five to twelve; teens through twenty-one; Main Choir, twenty-two to forty; Senior Choir, over forty; and Men's Choir. Practice rotated and was scheduled for the choir that would sing on the coming Sunday. Sometimes, on special occasions, the choirs would all sing mixed together, concert style. The choir was the pride of the church, and no celebration was complete without a choir participating. As a member of the choir, you could and would be called upon by an elder or minister to sing at any time, and you'd better be ready.

The church was about a fifteen-minute walk from our house. It too had been built in the neighborhood tradition by the folks who used it. Community meetings, weddings, funerals, most birthday parties, holiday celebrations, barbecues, and cookouts were all held at church.

It was the place everyone went to barter and swap goods on Saturday, what today we would call a flea market. There was a row of picnic tables covered with an A-frame roof to protect you from the sun and rain. On Saturdays, everyone would display what they had available for trade. Easy credit was available. They'd just say, "I know where you live," and that was your bond. There would be picnics, hide-and-go seek, bolo bat, hopscotch, and dodge ball going on all day. On Saturdays, church was fun!

THE GENERAL STORE AND THE POST OFFICE

FOLKS IN THE NEIGHBORHOOD PICKED UP THEIR FEW NEEDS at the two stores within walking distance, about half a mile away. Mr. Reeder's store also contained the post office. Mr. Whitehurst's store was where my grandmother had credit, so we always went there. I remember going to the store only for sugar or thread. We didn't really go shopping because we grew everything we ate in our own little neighborhood. Everything we didn't grow, we bartered for with others in the neighborhood. Whatever we got from the store we just signed for. Money changed hands only once a month when my grandma went to Mr. Whitehurst's store herself to pay her bill, with me at her side, of course. If Grandma was unable to go, I was sent with the money to "conduct the business" with one or both of my brothers sent along for protection because I was carrying Grandma's money. The bill was usually seven or eight dollars a month.

We did not buy from or have credit at Mr. Reeder's store because Grandma didn't want to "put all her eggs in one basket." Since Mr. Reeder had owned the eight acres of land my grandpa and uncles had worked as sharecroppers, Grandma refused to "give that man back money earned from the land we already gave our sweat for." We'd already paid him once. Therefore, we went to Mr. Reeder's store only to use the post office. Even that irritated my grandma, because the Reeders would know who was sending her mail or when one of my uncles from up north sent her a money order or when we got a package from Sears Roebuck or Montgomery Ward.

Grandma felt that was more information than they were entitled to know about her. This was evidence that they had forgotten she was no longer beholden to them. Her debt was paid. Her husband and sons had worked off the debt of the land. Grandma would carefully inspect every letter and package before opening it to determine if it had been tampered with. Sometimes she would find telltale signs that showed where a letter or package had been opened and resealed, no matter how carefully it was done. To Grandma, this meant "they knew as much about my business as I do." She hated their invasion of her privacy, but she loved to catch them at their game. To us she'd rant, rave, and exclaim about what she was going to do and say to them now that we had the deed to our land. She was going to "give them a piece of my mind." Remember, Grandma was born into slavery. In the world she came from, Colored folks just didn't confront or argue with white folks. So she never actually said anything to the Reeders, though that was hard to tell when you heard her tell the story.

The two stores sat diagonally across the road from one another, separated by the railroad tracks. In order to get to either one of them from our neighborhood, everyone had to walk along the path beside the ditch that separated Aunt Sadie's yard from ours and then through the cornfield behind our house. After that, for the next quarter mile the path was a cool oasis shielded from the sun by a tree canopy overhead. There was even a small flowing stream that ran under the footbridge and over into the big runoff ditch. It could be heard babbling most of the way. The footbridge at the big ditch always flooded over when it rained. Another few feet and we were out of the wooded path onto the road in the white neighborhood. This is where the white kids would gather and wait for us. They would throw rocks at us and yell, "Git back in them woods you niggers. Ya'll know monkeys like you ought to stay in the jungle."

We'd yell back, "Come on over here and make me, you soda cracker." This went on for generations, just a game of "chicken bluff" between friendly rivals. Very seldom was anyone actually hit by a rock because some of our parents worked for some of their parents and we'd all get a whipping if anyone got hurt or they found out. Whenever there were grown-ups around, we all played together and got along just fine.

Grandma never charged for what she thought of as her missionary work. However, people would always bring her something "for her trouble," a piece of fabric for quilting, a jar of homemade jelly or jam, a freshly baked pie, or flowers from their garden. It didn't really matter. They simply wanted to show their appreciation for her help and kindness and concern. Many said they did not know which of her services they treasured most—her prayers or her potions.

My brothers and sister were all younger than I was so I was right away cast in the role of assistant mother. My mother worked all the time, and Grandma needed an assistant. I was often in training as an apprentice for chores like washing the family laundry outside in the big round galvanized tub, making ice-cream on the back porch, cooking and kitchen chores, cleaning the house, supervising the wood gathering, cutting, and stacking. I worked under the supervision of my grandma. My siblings worked under my supervision. This was so true that if one of them did something improper, I would be the one punished. This made me super critical of everything they did, and, in general, mean as hell.

NAMES

My birth certificate records my name as Lorraine Sandra Tryphaena Ferebee. Mama named me Lorraine. Since she wasn't married when I was born, I took her maiden name as my last name, my grandma's last name, Ferebee. Aunt Sadie, who lived next door, named me Sandra; that's my second first name or would it be my first middle name? Grandma gave me my second middle name, Tryphaena. ("Greet those workers in the Lord, Tryphaena and Tryphosa." In Paul's letter to the Romans [16:12, ESV] he sent salutations to Tryphaena because she had served the church so faithfully.) My trouble with having too many names goes back to my beginning.

On my first day of school, I inserted a "u" in my name because it sounded richer and stronger to me than Sandra. I declared myself to be Saundra Ferebee. I wouldn't use my real first name because I couldn't stomach the way it was pronounced by everyone— "Loreen." That was a lot of fixing for a six-year-old. I got started early. At home, in the neighborhood, and at church, I was Lorraine. In school, I was Saundra.

As to my last names, after my second marriage, I had to finally stop using my maiden name, Ferebee. It was just too ridiculous to use four last names. As my career grew, I had to keep adding names. I have most often continued to use the last name of my first husband, Code. Not because of any affinity for him, but in acknowledgment of my two sons and grandchildren who carry that name.

Cabell was the last name of my second husband to whom I was married for fifteen years. It is the name I had in equestrian school and the name I used when graduating from the Alexander Foundation and the Feldenkrais® Awareness Through Movement training. I used the name on the road too when I traveled and taught Centered Riding Clinics in the United States, England, and Germany. It was also the name I taught under at Delaware Valley College in Doylestown, Pennsylvania.

Whitley is the last name of my third husband. Although I left Norfolk and went to Boston with him in 1966, we would not marry until many years later. I had not seen or heard from him in over forty-five years, when one day in 2010, my best friend Tina and I googled his name just for fun. Much to our surprise, we found him living in New York. I was living in Florida at the time. I went for a visit, and we decided to get married and pool our resources, which would help both of us financially. I didn't have any place I really wanted to be, and I thought New York would be fun. He was having health issues and needed help keeping up with his medications and finances. We got married and traded services. That's how we saw it at the time.

Inasmuch as I graduated from school, was credentialed, and had a twenty-year career in the equestrian field as Code and/or Cabell, I am compelled to include those names here. Rest assured, though, I will always be Lorraine Ferebee.

SCHOOL

WHEN I STARTED ELEMENTARY SCHOOL, IT DIDN'T TAKE Miss Freeman long to decide that I asked too many questions. Her solution to this problem was to send me to the library to help out. This was just fine with me, so I continued to ask too many questions. There was another girl, Ruth Clementina Schofield (who would become known to me as Tina), who was in a similar predicament. We became fast friends and still today we are best friends. She was beautiful, very shapely, and light skinned with long jet-black straight hair. She came from a family of financial means. I was tall and skinny with hair that was even too short to make a ponytail. We were the odd couple right from the beginning. When it came to looks and means, she had too much, and I had too little. So we comforted each other and provided each other with a shield from the barbed tongues of our classmates. We studied together and got good grades until the eighth and ninth grades when boys started to notice Tina and follow her around asking for dates.

Her mom and dad started allowing her to go out with boys when she was fifteen. By the time she was sixteen, she had her own car—a baby-blue Chevrolet convertible with a beige leather top and upholstery. I would be grinning from ear to ear when she came to pick me up at home or gave me a ride back home after school. Her body was well developed about the hips and breasts. She had the hourglass figure you saw in all the magazines. I, on the other hand, had nothing. I was as straight as a stick with neither hips nor breasts. Of course, I desperately wanted the boys to notice me too. They did. They all wanted me to play basketball on their team because

I always got the rebounds. No one was interested in having a date with "Slim," as I was called.

I was very popular and very smart academically, except where numbers were involved—algebra, calculus, and the like. I was class president, captain of the drama team, a cheerleader, drum major of the band, and I sang in the choir, not all at once, but between the eighth and eleventh grade.

The impact Union Kempsville Elementary and High School had on my life endures even today. I learned early on what success felt like. I learned from Miss Freeman what praise felt like. I learned from Miss Evelyn Smith what encouragement felt like. I learned from Mrs. Siler how to challenge myself and overcome what initially I had thought to be failure. I learned from Mr. Thaddeus Smith that the body and the brain work best when employed together. My experiences with these wonderful, inspiring educators taught me to think of myself as capable, as an achiever, a winner, a person who would not accept failure without a fight. My teachers had me convinced that I was smart and talented, a real go-getter who could do anything I set my mind to. I believed them, and I owe much of my success to adopting their expectations of me as my own. Throughout my life, through many different changes, many relocations (part of the equestrian career track), European travel, and training and travel throughout the United States, it has been the recognition I received in elementary and high school that I sought to replicate.

Getting to go on a date was a different story. I spent months begging, crying, pouting, and doing extra chores, until Mother talked my grandma into letting me go on a double date with Tina when I turned sixteen. My mother had not been allowed to date unsupervised until she was twenty-five years old. My grandma was afraid "she'd come to no good" and get pregnant out of wedlock, which she did anyway. My mother claimed I had come into being because she had not been allowed to date until she was too old to be chosen by anyone worthwhile. Using me as evidence that Grandma's strategy did not work, she won the argument. At this same time, Tina let it be known at school that if you wanted to go out on a date with her, you had to have a date for me too. She would only double date with me. God bless her!

I had only one real boyfriend in high school—Sherman Lewis. I was fourteen when we met, and I wasn't allowed to date yet. We saw each other only at the swimming hole and had just gotten to the hand-holding stage when I lost him. Although I can no longer remember what he looked like, I do remember his eyes were gray brown. I remember the headline in the local newspaper: BOY, 19, DROWNS IN SANDPIT. At that time, "Colored people" were not allowed to swim in the ocean off Virginia Beach. The Army Corp of Engineers from Fort Story excavated sand to make cement, creating large holes in the ground. Over time these large lake size holes filled up with rainwater. They were used by the Colored kids for swimming.

About fifteen of us kids were swimming, splashing, and playing in the sand pit when some kind of underground disturbance occurred. Sherman Lewis and one other kid disappeared in a whirlpool that erupted on that day. I learned that Sherman was nineteen from the newspaper article. He did not go to my school. We had met the summer before at the sandpit.

I remember the funeral vaguely. Lots of kids crying and me staring at the two shoeboxes on the table that were supposed to represent them. I was too stunned to cry. I just sat there wondering why this had happened to "me," not how it had happened to "him." I grieved for years. It was quite a shocking way to lose my first love.

SAUNDRA CODE

I was seventeen years old when I was asked out on a date by a twenty-seven-year-old guy whose name was Curtis Code. He was the best buddy of Tina's boyfriend, Ducky. I was still not getting any uncoerced dates at school, so I jumped at the chance. After months of begging and pleading with Mom and Grandma, I was finally allowed to go out on a double date with Tina and Ducky. Curtis and Ducky had driven out to the country from Norfolk to pick up high school girls for a fast evening of fun. Because they had a car, some booze, and were actually grown men, I was elated. I just knew my ship had finally come in.

Usually, after the football game on Friday nights, we would go to the local Colored beach, Seaview Beach, to neck and make out, which was taking on more and more interest for me. Curtis was quite experienced and eager to show me the way. After a few beers and cigarettes, before long necking turned into full-blown intercourse in the back seat of the car and eventually progressed to a blanket on the sand. I was thrilled. I'd heard the girls in school talking about how far they'd let their guy go. I felt so happy for my man that he got to go all the way. Talking about "leading a lamb to slaughter." I really was that stupid. Naive would be an understatement.

It took about four months before I was pregnant. Somehow, in my seventeen-year-old wisdom, the risk of getting pregnant always seemed smaller than the consequences of saying no and losing Curtis's affection and attention. I had not even asked him if he wore a condom. I didn't even know what one looked like. Wrong. This, of course, meant that I had to drop out of school, mandatory for the girl during that generation. I also had to tell my mother.

I was standing behind and almost underneath the long, black, pot-bellied stovepipe in the dining room. Mom was on the other side of the stove. We both had washbasins half full of water warming on top of the stove, readying for our morning wash-up before getting dressed for the day. "Mom," I said, "I haven't had my period for a couple of months, and I think I'm pregnant."

She upset her basin of water but said nothing for some time. Tears were running down her cheeks as she turned her head from side to side in the gesture of no, no, no and said, "ump, ump, ump... don't tell me, you too," referring to her own history with me. Sadly, Grandma was right again. Mom's immediate concern was how and when we were going to tell my grandma and her likely reaction. Although I had not yet recognized it, my mother knew what this meant. I would have to leave Grandma's house immediately. Her standing in the church, neighborhood, and community would demand no less. I must be made an example. It must be made clear to all that this behavior was unacceptable and punishable by shunning and dismissal. We had to find a solution before Grandma found out.

The obvious solution: marry the baby's father. I didn't know that he was living with his girlfriend and their two children at the time. It was February 1960, and I was having a baby. When my mother told my grandma about my pregnancy, she also told her about my wedding plans. That was all well and good, but Grandma still wanted me out of the house and out of her sight as soon as possible. She saw me as a failure. I had embarrassed her and her good name in both the church and the community, just as my mother had. She wanted no more part of me, she said.

Curtis was not happy about this new development either and tried to avoid the whole situation. He reluctantly agreed to marry me but did not participate in any of the planning or tell his family about me.

Tina and I planned the wedding. It was December when I learned I was pregnant, February when I told my mother, and May when I was to be married. A lot was happening during this time. I dropped out of school, too embarrassed to be seen, and besides, I had a wedding to plan. The wedding was planned for 6 p.m. on a Saturday at Lynnhaven Baptist Church, of course. Uncle and Auntie, across the road from our house, had everything ready for the wedding reception.

Tina, my maid of honor, and I were upstairs dressing for the wedding. We were having difficulty because my dress didn't fit. I was wearing my neighbor Clarice's prom dress as my wedding gown. Though I had tried it on just the week before and I wasn't even showing yet, the dress was now too tight, and we were struggling to get the zipper up when Clarice came running across the field saying I had an emergency phone call. We ran back across the field to her grandma's house where the phone was, me in my underwear covered only by a billowing flowery housecoat. After a few minutes, I returned, running back across the field to the house screaming and crying. I bolted upstairs with Mom and Tina following. I flung myself on the bed hysterically screaming over and over again, "He's not coming!"

The organist at church was notified and made the dreaded announcement. "Ladies and gentlemen, I regret to inform you that the groom has been unavoidably detained, and the wedding will be postponed." Word came back to the house that the church slowly began to empty out. All my classmates and teachers from school and folks from my neighborhood, everybody exited the church in a strange, stunned silence, most of them ending up at Uncle and Auntie's house where the reception was to have taken place. Someone had to eat all that food and drink all that champagne, and what to do with the wedding gifts? What does "postponed" mean? Leave the gifts or not?

Everybody went temporarily crazy trying to guess what had happened. Too embarrassed to be seen by anyone, I stayed hidden upstairs in my room, being consoled by Tina and my mom. Finally, my dad talked Mom into going to Norfolk to Curtis's mother's house to see if he was there. Dad was intent on finding him and making him "do the right thing." So off to Norfolk we went with several cars following the "best man" Ducky. Apparently, he was the only person Curtis told about the wedding. Ducky led us to Outten Street where Curtis's mother lived. Curtis was there. He answered the door in an unbuttoned tuxedo shirt and underwear, crying. His mother stood there totally confused about what was going on. She had not even been told that a wedding was supposed to occur. She knew nothing.

After quite a bit of explanation from me and Mom, and my dad pointing out to him that I was seventeen and he was twenty-seven, ten years my senior and headed to jail for statutory rape if he did not "do the right thing," he confessed and admitted his guilt. Even though it was after 10 p.m., his mother, Miss Helen, called her minister, and the whole gang followed her to the minister's house. We were married by two people I had never seen or spoken to before. In my mind's eye, I can still see the minister in his pale-blue print pajamas and navy-blue robe. His wife in her pink gown and matching robe sat at the piano playing the Wedding March at 11:30 p.m. Afterward, as we stood on the minister's porch with the three parents congratulating each other on the success of "getting the job done," Ducky asked Curtis, "Where you guys gonna spend the night?" Ducky had not only led us to Miss Helen's house, he had also been present to perform his duty as best man. As I was hugging everyone goodbye and receiving congratulations, Ducky was offering us the use of his rented room for our honeymoon night.

Curtis and I followed him to the rooming house. The room was on the second story of a four-story house owned by his father. The bathroom was one floor above or below, none on the second floor. The room was filthy. The walls had crumbling wallpaper, which had been torn and patched with newspapers for years. The sheets on the bed were a grayish brown, darker than my skin, although you could vaguely tell they had once been white. There was no other bedding in the room. The floors and all other surfaces were covered with several layers of dirty clothes. There were empty food containers and beer cans all about. If you allowed the room to grow dark, when you turned the light on, the walls came alive with roaches. It almost looked as though the walls themselves were moving. If you slept, you had to do so with the lights on and sitting up.

Curtis and Ducky dropped me off at the rooming house and went to get champagne to celebrate the wedding. After they left, I tried to remain standing because I didn't want to touch anything in that nasty room. After a couple of hours when they had not returned, I finally moved all the clothes off the only wooden chair in the room and placed it in the middle of the room. In that way I could see the roaches and mice before they were actually crawling on me. I sat there until daylight. Around noon, it finally began to dawn on me that Curtis wasn't coming back. I still just sat there. I had my purse and the overnight bag I had packed full of sexy clothes for my honeymoon, but I had no money, not one cent. Shortly after dark, Ducky appeared. He did not seem surprised that Curtis was not there or that I had not heard from him since they left together the night before. He showered downstairs, changed clothes, and went out again as though I was invisible.

After he left, I finally took off my wedding dress and changed into my one other outfit. I walked to the nearest busy intersection and spent the next hour trying to jump out in front of an oncoming bus or truck. I kept jumping off the curb into the oncoming traffic and then losing my nerve and jumping back onto the curb just in time. I wanted to die. I had sex before marriage. I was pregnant out of wedlock, just like my mother, and the man responsible cared so little he didn't even show up for the wedding. I had been abandoned in a rooming house on my wedding night. I had no money and nowhere to go and I was hungry and thirsty. Seventeen, penniless, homeless, and unwanted. Oh well, since my plan to commit suicide hadn't worked out, it was time for plan B. I did not call my family and tell them I had been deserted, abandoned. I was too embarrassed and ashamed and did not want to hear my grandma's "I told you so." I also didn't want the pitying looks of my mother, siblings, and friends. Only Tina knew the truth.

I called Miss Helen. Ducky had given me her phone number the night of the wedding. She was not surprised to hear from me. Yes, I could come and stay with her until I could work something else out. Unlike me, she had known about Curtis's girlfriend and the children before she took us to her minister to be married. She had expected this outcome. I stayed there until July and was the family's maid. Miss Helen would leave me a list of chores daily. Curtis's older sister, who still lived at home, would give me her list of chores to do also. After two months of this, I could take it no longer. Clarice had married a guy whose father was the director of public housing in Norfolk. I called her and asked for her help, telling her what my circumstances were.

Although Clarice told me her father-in-law said the waiting list for an apartment was about two years, within the week, she called and invited me to coffee at the diner around the corner from Miss Helen's house. I arrived first and she came in shortly after, dangling keys to 364 East Brambleton Avenue, my new apartment. She had pleaded with her father-in-law on my behalf. He had broken the rules skipping me ahead on the list, and even gave me two months free rent in exchange for cleaning and painting the apartment myself.

It was a two-bedroom apartment with a bathroom on the second floor, kitchen, dining area, and living room on the first floor. I moved in immediately saying a hasty thank you to Miss Helen. My furnishings were one straight-back wooden chair, twin-size mattress, one blanket, a plate, spoon, fork, knife, cup, and glass, all supplied by Tina. At seven months pregnant, I started painting the apartment, and that's what I was doing when my water broke. I took a cab to the hospital. On August 16, 1960, my son Deon Donnell Code was born prematurely when I was eight months pregnant.

While I was pregnant and living with Miss Helen, I had found a job at a dry cleaner in Virginia Beach. I still had to continue my chores at Miss Helen's house, but I had to earn some actual cash if I was ever going to leave her house. I took the bus from Norfolk to Virginia Beach five days a week. I had started sharing the morning paper with a very handsome, well-dressed, older man who worked at the golf and country club. His conversation was noteworthy and interesting: politics, Black pride, and the stock market. He even seemed to think I was intelligent enough to have conversations and debates about these things. His name was Frank Oliver, and he started handing me sections of his newspaper after he had read them. The bus ride was about an hour. He seemed nice but distant at first. Over the next few weeks and months, we began to talk more, and he began to befriend me. First coffee and donuts on the bus. Soon after that came dinner and cognac in my apartment. It soon became every day and everything: groceries, drinks, clothes, furniture, and though I was pregnant, sex all the time too.

I couldn't believe he found me attractive, pregnant with someone else's child. He was gentle with me and always considerate of my condition. I desperately wanted to do something for him to show my appreciation for his generosity, and sex was all I thought I had to give and what I thought he wanted from me. I was actually happy to oblige. At the time I really didn't know the difference between just sex and genuine lovemaking. I thought because he wanted me sexually, he loved me. I think he just felt sorry for me, alone, seventeen, pregnant, and living in a near empty apartment.

When my son Deon was born, he weighed only four pounds and two ounces and had to remain in the hospital after I was released. His lungs were not completely formed, and he was unable to breathe on his own. On the second day Mom went with me to see Deon. The doctor called me in for a consultation. I was told that my son would not survive, and it was best that I didn't get too attached to him. The doctor recommended that I not visit but once or twice a week. Since I was told he wasn't going to survive anyway, we asked if I could take him home where he would be comforted by loving arms until his time came. The request was presented to and discussed with the attending physician who gave us his blessing. I left the hospital with Deon Donnell Code when he was five days old.

My mother told Grandma the condition Deon was in, and she asked that we both be brought to her. When we left the hospital, my mother drove us directly to Grandma's house. Grandma took one look in the blankets and fell to her knees crying and lamenting in prayer. She then picked him up very, very gently and held him in one hand. She held his head in her fingertips and his butt on the heel of that hand. She asked for a pillow and placed him in the center. She carried that pillow in her arms everywhere she went for the next six weeks.

Grandma took complete charge of my son. She prepared all his food and fed him herself every time he ate. She gave him food in his drugstore formula, and as he grew older, she added applesauce, oatmeal, and mashed potatoes to the bottle. She also gave him some of the potions made from the plants I used to gather in the woods for her. She bathed him and changed all his diapers herself so she could inspect his poop to see if it looked healthy. She took him outside on his pillow for fresh air daily, walking him about the neighborhood. No matter how angry, disappointed, and ashamed of me she had been when I first announced my pregnancy, she forgot all about that when she saw what condition my baby was in. Had it not been for her, Deon would not have survived. I had no experience taking care of an infant not to mention one that weighed less than five pounds. I was actually scared to hold him. He was so small I thought I might hurt him. When he was six weeks old, Grandma let me take him home. He weighed eight pounds.

FRANK OLIVER

WHILE DEON WAS BEING CARED FOR BY MY GRANDMA, Frank moved into the apartment permanently and decided that I shouldn't work anymore. He wouldn't hear of me going back to the cleaners in Virginia Beach where I worked when we met. He said I needed to be home to take care of Deon when Grandma let me bring him home. This was true and so I gratefully stayed home.

Frank was twenty-two years older than I was and satisfied my long-held desire for a father. In addition to being a provider, he was also my lover and protector. I loved him fiercely, and he took immediate and complete charge of me, the household, and my comings and goings. Fifteen months later, I was pregnant again. By this time, I had become captive in my own home and wasn't allowed to leave the apartment without his permission. His possessiveness and the isolation this caused had begun to trouble me. He just couldn't believe that I could love someone so much older than I was.

In addition to being a golf caddy, Frank was also a numbers runner. He took small bets from the locals and placed them uptown with the bosses. When the numbers came out in his favor, meaning he didn't have to pay out a lot to the local winners, I'd get a take-out restaurant dinner, cocktails, good sex, and a wonderful evening. If the payout was big, meaning too many people hit the number on the same day, he'd get really mad, drink a lot, come home, and beat my ass. It was a well-practiced ritual.

After two years of this repeated behavior, I started devising a plan to leave Frank. Because of the expected increase in expenses with the new baby coming, Frank finally relented and allowed me to go back to work. I took and passed the civil service test for Clerk II and went to work at the library on the naval base; that is, whenever I wasn't too bruised up or didn't have a black eye, swollen face or lips. I started secretly hiding a little money from each paycheck that I would someday use to leave. However, before I could follow through on my plan, and eighteen months after my second son, Frank Vincent, was born, I discovered I was pregnant again.

Frank was elated but I now was really trapped. I was twenty-one years old with almost three children and a very possessive, violent man on my hands. Deon had survived and was doing quite well. Vincent was smart, healthy, and happy. Angel Maria, my beautiful little girl, arrived fifteen months after Vincent. Nothing was the same after Angel was born. I had hoped each time I was pregnant to have a girl, and finally, here she was, "my" Angel.

Frank had started to abuse the children too. His favorite way to hurt me was to lock the children in their bedroom and not allow me to feed them or take care of their needs in any way. I knew I had to find a way to get away from him and the sooner the better. I had a daughter to protect now. With money from my job, I bought a car. It was an old 1954 Ford Fairlane. It wasn't much to look at, but it ran well.

I'd never told anyone in my family about the abuse, only Tina knew. Frank told me he'd kill us all if I did, and I believed him. He'd come close several times already. So I decided to go for broke. I decided that the next time he hit me I would fight back until one of us was no longer standing. At this point, I was living with so much fear and pain that I really didn't care who won. If he won and killed me, I wouldn't have to figure out how to raise three kids by myself. If I won and he went down, I could do whatever I damn well pleased while I figured it out. So I'm all in!

I got my chance before long. I was sitting on the sofa holding Angel on my lap when Frank came home. The boys were outside playing. He was drunk, which meant he'd had to make a big payout, so I knew this meant I was in trouble. There was a coffee table in front of the sofa, and sitting on it was a piece of driftwood shaped like a duck with a long neck and beak. Artificial flowers protruded from the tail end of the duck. Frank leaned over the coffee table and slapped me across the face and said, "Get up bitch and come here." I lay Angel on the sofa, picked up the duck by its neck and clubbed him in the head. Because he was drunk and my response had been so quick and unexpected, he lost his balance and fell to the floor. I seized the opportunity, straddled him on the floor with the duck still in my hand, and pummeled him into unconsciousness. The neighbors heard the screaming, followed by complete silence, and broke through the screen door. They were surprised to find it was Frank who was screaming and crying this time. They had expected it to be me as the kids and I had taken refuge in many of their homes over the three years we had been there.

It took several neighbors to pull me off him. They seemed relieved that it was Frank who was taking the abuse this time. I had at least two years of pent-up anger and rage, and it was taking a while for me to work it all out. By the time the medics arrived, he had regained consciousness. He told them he had been jumped, beaten, and robbed by a group of teenagers while waiting at the bus stop. They didn't believe him. They had responded to too many domestic violence calls at this address in the past. As they took him away to the hospital, siren blaring, I knew this was the chance I had been waiting for, my chance to get away from him.

I didn't know where I was going, but I knew I had to be gone when he got out of the hospital. His sister came to visit me on the second day of his hospitalization. She had been to visit him, and like me she knew he would retaliate. She brought me $500 in cash and asked me to please get out of the apartment before he got out of the hospital. She didn't want to see him spend the rest of his life in jail for killing me. She knew how violent his temper could be, having experienced it herself.

JOHN ANTHONY (TONY) WHITLEY

A COUPLE OF YEARS EARLIER, MY NEIGHBOR AND BABYSITTER, Virginia, had introduced me to one of her husband's friends, Tony Whitley. Tony and Virginia's husband, Garris, worked at the post office together. Tony was married and had children. He had just recently bought a house in a neighboring town for his family. We had acknowledged the spark between us when we met, but we didn't act on our attraction. He was trying to make a go of it with his wife for the sake of their kids, or so he said. I was scared to death of Frank and already had three small kids, so I wasn't ready to get involved again. Tony eventually left the post office. He and his wife and kids moved to Boston.

When I left Frank, I had packed up everything in the apartment so I could move quickly as soon as I found another place. The first place I found I moved out of as quickly as I moved in. In the middle of the night I found mice in my daughter's crib when she woke me up crying. That night the kids and I slept in a homeless shelter. I was getting used to moving—good thing.

By this time, Tony and his wife were in the process of getting a divorce. He came back to Norfolk to visit Garris and Virginia just before I put Frank in the hospital. Each day when I went to pick up my kids after work, he would engage me in conversation and encourage me to stay and make the card game a foursome. That didn't work out because I had never learned to play cards. It was forbidden in my grandma's house. He had kept up with my circumstances through Virginia and Garris and knew all about the violence and abuse. When he heard the story of how Frank came to be in the hospital and the plans Frank had for me when he got out, Tony suggested I pack up my kids and belongings and go back to Boston with him. I'm sure he was only half sincere, joking. He never expected me to actually say yes and go to Boston with him. But in the dead of winter, January 8, 1966, we rented a U-Haul trailer, attached it to the old Ford Fairlane, and set out following Tony to Boston. It was snowing like hell from Virginia to Boston as we drove. The weather was colder than anything I had ever experienced before. I was, after all, a southern girl. It was 13 degrees when we arrived in Boston.

I really didn't know Tony at all. Aside from having a crush on him, I knew nothing except that he was handsome and well dressed, drove a fancy car, and talked really fast. He talked so fast that most people couldn't understand what he was saying. He thought I was wonderful because I could. He was very gentle and kind with me. After living with Frank and the consequent physical, sexual, and emotional abuse, I was overwhelmed by Tony's generosity. We had not yet made love when we arrived in Boston, and I was eager to totally belong to this new and seemingly wonderful man who had rescued me.

It was "out of the frying pan into the fire" when we arrived in Boston. Tony took us to this huge house on the corner of Blue Hill and Geneva Avenues in Dorchester. The house was surrounded by a four-foot-high stone wall and beautiful snow-covered shrubs and trees. It had a wraparound porch on three sides. The beautiful, ornate, hand carved double front doors swung open immediately, and we were greeted by a well-endowed woman in a maid's uniform. She greeted us enthusiastically, said her name was Sylvia, and quickly ushered us through the vestibule and down a winding staircase to the basement. I followed behind her carrying Angel with Deon and Vincent following me. We were all exhausted, and I was almost in a daze after driving for sixteen hours, most of the way in the snow, with no prior experience driving on icy, slippery roads.

The basement was set up dormitory style with bunk beds along one wall, enough for ten or twelve kids to sleep. There was a classroom and library area with a teacher and four very attentive students already involved in their studies for the day. When my children entered the room, all the kids ran to greet them, and the teacher announced they would break for lunch and get acquainted with the new arrivals. The teacher suggested I leave my children with her for lunch and go check out the rest of the house above. The place was spotless and orderly, and the food smelled so good that I did not hesitate to take her up on her offer. I was excited and eager to see the rest of the house. My adrenalin kicked in, and Sylvia began the tour. I couldn't believe my good fortune. It seemed by the looks of the house and my surroundings that Tony was rich.

When Sylvia and I emerged from the basement stairwell, we entered a very large room with a bar at the far end. I had been whisked downstairs so quickly when we first arrived that I had not noticed any of the details of this room. Several very beautiful, partially clad girls were perched provocatively on bar stools. Some were modeling lingerie for a group of well-dressed businessmen who would take lingerie home to their wives. The customers were encouraged to feel the fabric, if they liked, while the models lingered.

We exited that room by way of another winding staircase rising to the second floor. There were eight rooms on this floor. All the rooms were decorated completely different from one another and had adjoining bathrooms. Each one was more beautiful than the next. You could also continue through the bathroom to the next bedroom when invited. By now, even I was beginning to understand the nature of the residence. Its purpose had suddenly become crystal clear, and so had Tony's purpose for inviting me to live with him in Boston.

The third floor was Tony's private quarters. It was one large round room with windows all around. There were fourteen windows. In places where you could see out, between the fronds of the Boston ferns that hung in front of each window, you could see only the treetops and the sky. Everything in the room was beautiful. Persian rugs adorned the glistening dark hardwood floor, along with chairs and sofas covered in a pale-blue velvet brocade. Sylvia let me know that each night one lucky girl got to spend the night with Tony. As a welcome to me, "the new girl," all the girls had decided that I would have the honor that night.

I delighted as I sat in the whirlpool bathtub in Tony's quarters. It was large enough to accommodate up to six people. Elsa, one of the girls modeling lingerie when I'd entered the great room on the first floor, was sent to give me a massage after my bath. She brought with her, and dressed me in, the finest lingerie I had ever seen. As she had been giving me a massage, Sylvia had done likewise with Tony. Both girls lit candles and turned back the bed covers as they left the room.

Tony then explained to me how things worked. Each girl saw four Johns, five days a week, with two days off each week and two weeks paid vacation a year. He paid all the bills, bought the girls work clothes (lingerie), and provided health care, beauty shop expenses, manicures and pedicures, cosmetics, toiletries, food, liquor, pot, cocaine, and anything else within reason that any of the girls wanted. The girls received $100 a day for an allowance. Financial negotiations with the Johns were always handled by Tony or the bookkeeper. He wanted his girls to have everything they wanted. He wanted them to be happy.

NO! I COULD not do it. Actually, I WOULD not do it!

It wasn't that I could not sell my body. Strangely enough, I didn't think that was so bad. It was giving someone else the money that I couldn't abide. My body, my money. That's how I saw it. I found the idea of giving the money to someone else far more offensive and repugnant than the act itself. It was almost as if this had happened to me in another lifetime, something eerily familiar. Tony wanted to know what I thought my contribution to this union would be when I decided to come to Boston. I had to admit that I had not thought about that at all. I had only thought about getting out of town before Frank got out of the hospital. When Tony had said, "Why don't you go back to Boston with me?" and I said okay, I was as surprised as he was. Maybe I thought we would fall madly in love on the long drive in separate cars, and we would live happily ever after, huh?

I did spend the night with Tony that first night in Boston. We made sweet love all night. On January 12, 1966, four days after leaving Norfolk with my kids in the car and with the U-Haul trailer still attached, I moved to the parking lot of the Stop & Shop supermarket in Roxbury. It was 18 degrees outside. We would go to the library, wash-up in the bathroom, and then stay there all day to keep warm. The boys would babysit Angel, keeping her quiet while I went on job interviews. This lasted three days before the car and U-Haul were spotted by one of the girls from Tony's house.

Once he realized that I really wasn't going to work for him, he decided to treat me differently. He paid the rent for the first few months on a new apartment, which gave me time to find a job, schools, and child care for my kids. He took his evening meals with us every night and spent the night in my bed whenever he chose, which was often enough for me. He was ten years my senior, another father figure, and by this time I was completely in love with him. I had been rescued twice by him, but his womanizing and lifestyle eventually separated us for over forty-five years.

I found work at the Boston Public Library right away because of my experience working at the Norfolk Naval Base Library. After a few months, I was able to increase my salary substantially by moving to a job with Action for Boston Community Development, Inc. (ABCD). This community organization was part of the Kennedy/Johnson war on poverty. When ABCD was recruiting for federal civil service jobs in the community center where I worked as a job counselor, I recruited myself and was hired by the US Department of Labor, Manpower Administration, as a GS-7. From 1969 to 1984, fifteen years, I traveled to the ten regional office cities of the Labor Department, comparing numbers, planned versus actual, of economically disadvantaged people who found employment. It was an exciting time for me, and I loved getting to see so much of America. My job was to monitor the employment of minorities by state agencies throughout the New England states.

BILL RILEY

I MET BILL RILEY WHEN HE BECAME DIRECTOR OF AN AFTER school educational program for kids in the poorest part of Boston. My kids went to this program after school. He encouraged the parents of the kids to participate in the program whenever possible. I started attending some of the classes and particularly enjoyed the poetry writing class. Bill was an English teacher at a suburban high school, and this was volunteer work for him. He taught the poetry writing class himself. He was very handsome and held a doctorate from Harvard. An intellectual white man with access to the Harvard University Library. This was surely something out of the ordinary.

Bill was always reading, usually two and three books simultaneously. Therefore, I began to read everything and anything he left behind. I too had always loved books and having previously worked at two libraries, I needed little encouragement to get lost in the world of literature. Through our shared appreciation of books and literature and my efforts at poetry writing, we became close and began a romantic relationship. This was the first time I had ever been romanced. I was swept away by bouquets of flowers, expensive wines, and slow, gentle lovemaking designed to give me pleasure rather than to get pleasure for himself. He was also a photographer and encouraged my modeling ambition. He took pictures of me all over Boston and was instrumental in getting me signed with a modeling agency.

Before long, Bill moved into the apartment with me and my kids. He traveled to Virginia Beach with us and stayed at my grandma's house. Of course, my grandma had passed away by this time. She would never have allowed a white man to spend the night in her house. She would have been sure the nightriders would find out about it, and we would have to pay. I was very proud to bring home this handsome, well-educated man who openly showed his love and devotion to me and my children for all the world to see.

He was separated from his wife and kids, having left suburbia for a small apartment in the ghetto. Several times one or two of his kids came to spend the weekend with us. One summer his oldest son, sixteen at the time, came to spend the summer. They got into a heated argument, which resulted in some pushing and shoving and a few blows being passed between them. By this time, Bill was divorced and had asked me to marry him. I loved him very much but could not put the physical encounter I had witnessed between him and his son out of my mind. I was afraid that someday this could happen with one of my sons. I knew if it did, I would only see a white man flogging my Black son(s). I knew this would trigger scenes of slavery in my mind and I would come to the defense of my son, putting another man in the hospital. After I refused his proposal, our relationship deteriorated, and he moved out of the apartment. A few years later, I passed him on the street accompanied by a beautiful Black lady. He introduced me to his wife and new baby girl, the most beautiful olive-skinned, blue-eyed little girl I had ever seen. They were not only a good-looking family but a happy one as well. I was happy for him.

ANGEL MARIA CODE

ON MAY 28, 1968, ONE DAY BEFORE HER FIFTH BIRTHDAY, my little girl, Angel Maria Code, made her transition to another world. She had been hospitalized for stomach cramps and nausea. After two weeks in the hospital and all conceivable tests coming back negative, her doctors at Massachusetts General Hospital Pediatric Unit decided to release her for a few days, kind of a test run to see how she would do if released permanently to home care. No big deal. It's just going to take some time to figure this out.

We were all ecstatic. Angel was finally coming home. HURRAY! HURRAY! She seemed fine but weak. I kept her in bed surrounded by her favorite toys and doted on by her two loving brothers, although Vincent was definitely in charge. On her third day at home, things were going so well, I decided to go to work. The boys were babysitting Angel, and after lunch, all three kids took a nap together, at my suggestion. When the boys woke up and Angel didn't, they knew something was wrong. Vincent tried and tried but couldn't wake her up. When he called me at work, he said, "Mommy, I can't wake Angel up. I stuck her with a pin just a little bit, Mommy, and she did not move or even cry. I don't think she's breathing." She never woke up again.

Thank God, my office mate and good friend Thomasina ran out of the office behind me.

We hopped a cab and went flying through Roxbury at breakneck speed with the cab driver blaring his horn and flashing his lights repeatedly, but we still couldn't go fast enough. The neighbors had already called 911 and the ambulance was pulling up just as the cab arrived. This is where everything slows way down and seems to move in slow motion in my memory. All the sounds became muffled. I stepped out of my body and became void. I couldn't feel anything. All color disappeared and everything turned gray.

Still in slow motion, I ran upstairs to the bedroom and found Angel in bed. She wasn't breathing, but I couldn't connect that thought to the idea that she was dead. Not yet. I couldn't comprehend what was happening. Picking her up, I went running down the stairs with her in my arms and handed her over to the medic who was running up the stairs. We all jumped in the back of the ambulance, Thomasina included. The medics began CPR as we sped away to the city hospital.

As soon as we arrived, they took Angel into the emergency room, and the doctors made an incision in her chest in order to access her heart. There was so much confusion, and everything was moving so fast that they forgot I was there. I followed them into the examination room and saw them open my daughter's chest before I passed out. When I woke up there was a policeman waiting to see me. In Massachusetts, when a child dies at home, child abuse must be ruled out before they can release the body to a funeral home. I was so shocked I couldn't speak at all. My daughter was dead, and I was being arrested. Had it not been for Thomasina, my office mate who had followed me home, I can't imagine what would have happened. I literally could not talk. I could not even blink my eyes. I just sat there staring into space, silent, speechless, unable to move, unable even to cry. Thomasina told them about Angel having just been released from Massachusetts General Hospital Pediatric Unit. They contacted the hospital, talked to the doctors involved, gave me their condolences and those of the staff of doctors as well, and sent me home without my baby.

I became the most efficient funeral administrator ever. I didn't have time to grieve. I had work to do. I called everybody who needed to be called, made travel arrangements for my mom and everyone else. I chose the casket, clothes, music, and scripture. I refused to let anyone else participate in her service.

I played the music and read poetry. I was much too angry at God to even read the scripture I had chosen. How could God do this to me, take my Angel? It was Angel who was gone, but somehow, I felt like it was me who had died. I was sure God knew how much I loved my little girl, so why would He do a thing like this to me? What was it telling me? For a long time, I viewed Angel's death as something that happened to me rather than something that happened to her.

I sometimes still feel that way. For her there was no death, just another life.

One day about six months later, I set the table for dinner and set a place for Angel's plate. Vincent asked me, "Who's that plate for, Mom?" I became hysterical, crying for the first time. It took six months for me to cry. My heart still aches for her today. I stayed in Boston for another four years. After Angel passed away, nothing was quite the same. I lost my will to live. I missed her so much. I kept being plagued by what-ifs. What if I had not gone to work that day? Would I have noticed soon enough to save her? What if Vincent is forever scarred because he had to stick a pin in her? What if? What if?

I went through several short-term relationships over the next few years while in Boston. These relationships were usually with married men because those relationships were safe to me. No commitments. I couldn't get too serious or too close to someone who was married. I could keep my autonomy. I could be my own boss. I couldn't or wouldn't trust anybody and wouldn't let anyone get close to my children. I was devoted to working, often two or even three jobs at the same time. I was more determined than ever before to provide for my children, or maybe it was so that I would be too tired to feel the pain. They may not have had a dad, but they were going to have everything else.

There was one exception to not allowing the boys to meet the men I dated—General William L. Peterson. Though he too was married, he was a United States Air Force General, and I felt some exposure to an African American man of his caliber and stature would be good for the boys. We dated for over a year, and I even allowed him to take the boys on outings without me going along. He was very generous with them, often buying them toys and clothes and taking them on day trips. Though they may never have realized the connection, I've always felt that brief encounter had something to do with their desire to join the military after they graduated from high school, which they both did.

BOSTON TO CAPITOL HILL

For some years, my mother's health had been in decline. After driving sixteen hours at best from Boston to Virginia Beach, alone, several times with the kids asleep in the car, it became clear that I needed to be closer to home. The frequency of these trips was increasing, and I couldn't afford to fly myself and two children, let alone endure the physical toll and safety issues of driving that far alone. I requested a transfer from Boston to Washington, DC, which was only a four-hour drive from Virginia Beach. In 1973 I transferred from the US Department of Labor in Boston to the National Office in Washington, DC. The cost of the move was paid for by the US Department of Labor. Since working for the feds, I had been promoted several times and was now a GS-12, earning about $45,000 a year.

At first we moved to a new suburban model community known for its diversity—Reston, Virginia. It was beautiful and spotlessly clean. Quite different from our neighborhood in Roxbury. We lived in a two-bedroom apartment just off the golf course in the Lake Anne section of town. I took the commuter bus to Washington each day.

While riding the bus, I met a fellow passenger, Brenda Joyce, who told me about the Reston Riding Stable. She too had always wanted to learn to ride horses and was about to start taking lessons. What had fate wrought? I could hardly believe what my ears were hearing. It was music to my ears. Finally! Hallelujah! Thank you, Jesus! Access, a way to get on a horse, a way to fulfill my lifelong dream.

The first time I got on a horse I learned something unexpected. I was terrified. In all my imaginings of myself riding, I had always thought I would cause the horse to move. It had never occurred to me that the horse's movements would cause me to move too. I had not realized how much physical movement was involved for the rider. I had not seen balance as a concern, and being afraid had not once crossed my mind; but nothing can make you more afraid or cause you to loose trust more than constantly losing your balance while giving yourself over to something greater than yourself. Trust equals having enough confidence in yourself to believe that you can communicate with the horse and that you have the skill and prowess to demonstrate it, a demonstration of grace.

Riding a horse is not like absorbing any other form of movement because a horse can think, make independent decisions, and act on them. The rider must be able to intervene and redirect the horse's energy, actions, and intent and achieve a safe outcome should this occur. And it will. It can be caused by something as simple as the horse reacting to a piece of paper that blows in our direction.

The only defense that the horse has is to run. So when a horse senses danger, is surprised or frightened, he will run. If you are on his back, you must maintain your balance and composure. Much to my surprise, when the horse began to move, I froze and became rigid. I froze because of the myriad of physical sensations that overtook my body and came together as fear. I did not realize that riding was about trust on a different level than I had ever experienced before. It required two-way, nonverbal communication between an animal and a person. This is what would be required if we were both to be comfortable.

So I tried to pretend that I wasn't afraid, but the horses could feel the physical tension caused by my completely visceral response, and it transferred to them and made them nervous too. It took many years, professional help with body awareness, and a very special horse named Snaffles to overcome this problem. When you learn to ride for the first time at thirty-eight years old, you have many unconscious physical behaviors and habitual patterns. My first riding experience exposed my lack of body awareness, and it wasn't until I was introduced to Centered Riding that I understood this fully.

Once I discovered my seat bones and allowed my thighs and legs to softly drape around the horse's barrel, things got better; but this took a while. At first it felt like I was sitting on something substantial, something solid, but then it began to move, which caused my pelvis and legs to oscillate. I have felt fear of this caliber only once before when my brothers had poured a bag of big, fat, fuzzy brown caterpillars down between my shirt and skin. I was not only scared but repulsed enough to throw up. I wanted to get off immediately, but couldn't. I had waited too long for this moment to give up without a fight.

I joined Brenda and we began to take a group riding lesson once a week. Finally, I got my hands on a horse. I got to groom and tack up a horse and ride for one hour for $60, a bargain. That was confirmation. I had to ride. I had to learn more. Brenda and I still share stories of that time today. We remain close, as close as we can be while she has been living in Africa for the past twenty-five years. Our love of the horse is still a large part of our relationship.

The town of Reston was so new it didn't have a junior high school yet, and my kids were bused to the junior high school in the neighboring town of Sterling, Virginia. Sterling was a redneck town and the kids there had never seen the likes of the two ghetto thugs they thought my sons to be. One day one of the rednecks called Vincent a black nigger and "it was on." I spent more time in the principal's office at that school than the principal did himself. They couldn't seem to understand that I thought if someone called my son a black nigger, he was supposed to kick ass, or I would kick his ass. So I decided that it wasn't safe for my over 6′2″, 160-pound sons to go to school in Sterling, Virginia.

We moved from Reston, Virginia, to Capitol Hill and rented a three-story house on Randolph Place in the northwestern quadrant of Washington, DC. Living room, dining room, bathroom, and kitchen were on the first floor. Two bedrooms and a full bathroom were on the second floor. The third floor had one large room and a bathroom, and this became my bedroom. The house had two wood-burning fireplaces, one on the first floor and one on the third floor, and it had a large backyard.

The boys were enrolled in the nearby Dunbar High School. A few days in, they both came home all scraped up with bloody noses and raw knuckles, and minus their leather jackets and watches. Vincent said they were told they had to join a drug gang in order to go to that school, and they would continue to be robbed until they joined a gang, sold and used drugs, and thereby got protection. There were no free agents in that school. Join in or get out. It cost $750 a semester for each of them to go to Catholic School. The school gave me a partial scholarship for one of them because they thought they would play basketball. The boys entered Mackin Catholic High School.

When we moved to DC, I left the Reston Riding Stable, but I couldn't stop riding. It had become my therapy. It had never occurred to me that the greatest problem I would have learning to ride a horse had nothing to do with riding a horse but was all about controlling the solar plexus. I didn't even know I had a fear of falling until I started taking riding lessons at Great Falls Horse Center in Virginia. I soon learned that there was a professional riding school, Morven Park, an hour and a half west, in Leesburg, Virginia. As soon as I heard about this school, I knew it was my destiny, a two-year school all about horses. One of the instructors at Great Falls Horse Center, Louie Massinople, was a graduate of Morven Park. She was not what one would expect an equestrian to be like. She was short, squat, broad-shouldered, and loud-mouthed.

She was not patient with people, but with horses she had a gift. She was a natural. She was skilled, patient, gentle, and kind. When she told me how expensive Morven Park was—$7,500 a semester, $15,000 a year—I knew I couldn't afford it. It was clearly way out of my league. I don't know why, but that didn't slow down my intentions one bit. I just kept plodding along, one lesson a week with Louie. She loved to jump, and her specialty was training horses to jump. She always needed a guinea pig when she was training. Often, I was it. "Get up. Get back on," I can still hear her screaming. She also believed the best way to teach balance and get rid of fear was to ride without a saddle, which she usually had me do. She claimed that the perilous situations she put me in were to prepare me for the exam to get into Morven Park. I suppose she was right because it also taught me how to fall off a horse without breaking my neck. The emergency dismount is a truly valuable skill, which I did have occasion to use over the years.

Louie listened to my aspirations, and in spite of the fact that I was a forty-two-year-old Black woman with no experience and no money, she took me on anyway. Took me on and resolved to help me pass the admittance test for Morven Park. Ain't God good! After over two years of preparation, Louie gave me her blessing and the go-ahead to take the exam. We thought I'd have to take it more than once. We knew for sure that I wasn't ready for the last part of the exam, the canter without stirrups. I was terrified but compelled to find out what my other deficits were.

I was so scared that I told only Deon, Vincent, Tina, and Brenda, my old riding pal from Reston, that I was taking the exam. I didn't want to hear the usual "Are you crazy?" comments from the rest of my family.

When we moved from Boston to Reston, Virginia, the boys were thirteen and fourteen years old. I continued to work for the US Department of Labor for another few years until I saw an opportunity to parlay the skills I had learned there into a business venture. After fifteen years as a job analyst with the US Department of Labor, I resigned to open a consulting firm in Washington, DC, The Management Assistance Group, Inc. (MAGI).

I bought a house, employed fourteen people, and successfully contracted with state and local governments in the areas of job analysis, manpower administration, and organizational development. The MAGI conducted pre-audits of state and local statistics, monitoring the hiring of minorities before the Feds came in to inspect. We assisted with state efforts to pass the annual performance review. Deon and Vincent both worked for MAGI. They operated the copying machines and produced the training manuals that the MAGI sold and used to train clients. The business went into decline when the Democrats lost the presidential election, which resulted in minority contracts not being funded or renewed.

Within the next two years Deon and Vincent were both to graduate from Mackin Catholic High School and were preparing to join the military—Deon the Marine Corps and Vincent the Navy. I was preparing to take the admittance test for Morven Park, a professional riding school that prepared "young" men and women for careers in the equestrian arts. It was the place for Olympic hopefuls and was attended by the children of the wealthiest horse families in America, families who owned and bred America's finest sport horses. Students were mostly sixteen-to-twenty-year-olds. I was forty-two. All during this time, I'd say to my kids, "When you grow up and leave home, I'm going to riding school." Like my grandma, they too thought that to be a rather foolish ambition.

Meanwhile, it was becoming obvious that my mom was not going to survive her hospital stay. Near the end, as I sat by her bedside, day after day, her conversation would turn to what she wished she had done. She would talk about the opportunities she'd had to pursue her dreams which she didn't take, the chances she'd let slip through her fingers, the places she'd wanted to go but didn't, the things she'd wanted to experience, and then finally, the sorrow she now felt that she'd let it all pass by. She said, "Better to try and fail than fail to try." She couldn't remember who told her that, but she made me repeat it back to her several times and vow this would not happen to me. She did not want this to be the conversation I would be having with my kids at the end of my life.

SAUNDRA CODE CABELL

IT WAS ABOUT THIS TIME THAT I MET COVANCE CABELL. He was on vacation in DC, visiting my next-door neighbor at the MAGI, Betty Whaley. Betty was president of the Washington Urban League and quite the socialite. I had once worked for her as her administrative assistant after leaving the Feds. She had been instrumental in helping me obtain the business property next door to her townhouse on Capitol Hill for the MAGI. Her townhouse was a social mecca, the place to be to meet and greet Black society and politicians. Betty was being visited by an old college chum from Chicago, Ed Cabell. With him were his wife, Elaine, and son, Covance. Covance was an ex-semiprofessional football player and had quite the body, a big guy, 6′3″ and 235 pounds, muscular and attractive. His upper arms made my heart beat faster. They looked like those of Erin Neville, the Louisiana musician. Covance was a tennis buff and was hanging out at the neighborhood tennis courts enjoying his vacation.

One day he forgot his key and returned to Betty's unable to get back into the house. He came next door to my office to use the phone. I opened the door and sparks flew. His body was so beautiful, so robust, all that tennis. His smile was like the sun. I avoided him for several days knowing what was going to happen. He kept trying to see me and I kept telling my office staff downstairs to tell him I was out of the office. He was clever enough to wait until all my staff had gone home for the day, and then he rang the doorbell. When I opened the door, thinking it was UPS or FedEx, there he stood with this "I got you now" smile.

Within the hour, we were upstairs in my office on the floor under the big library table I used for my desk, making love. He went back to Chicago with his family after the vacation was over. Within a month, I went to visit him in Chicago. After a few visits back and forth for both of us, and meeting each other's families, we were married within a year. Our relationship was all about sex. We had mad passionate sex anywhere, at any time. We had little else in common. As for his ambitions, he was doing quite well. He had married the elusive president of the MAGI. Initially he was quite ambitious, but he had trouble keeping a job. He looked good, but his past sports success had not translated well in the nation's capital where the currency was vocabulary. He was not prepared for the political environment and the everyday lobbying that underlies acquaintances and relationships in Washington, DC.

Before Covance and I were married, I explained that when my sons joined the military, as they were planning to do upon graduation from high school, I was planning to go to Equestrian school for a year. He was very excited for me and supported the idea completely. He understood that this was a lifetime ambition. He planned to stay at my/our Capitol Hill townhouse and hold down the fort during the year I'd be away. Morven Park was only two hours away, and I could come home on weekends sometimes. His mom and I had many long discussions about my desire to work with horses. She did not laugh at me. In fact, when she passed away, she left me $5,000 in her will to help pay for riding school because she knew how important it was to me.

In October of 1983, my mom passed away. I had to decide if I really was going to Morven Park or if I was just whistling Dixie. What about my responsibility to my siblings? As the oldest child in the family, should I move back to Virginia Beach and maintain the homestead? As a single parent, my sole focus for almost twenty years had been providing for my sons' needs. I wanted to be all things to all people. I was very torn. Grandma was already gone, now Momma, and here, as Grandma would say, I was talking about "running away from home and family, to go do God knows what with horses, is she crazy!"

While I sat with Mama in the hospital during her last days, she and I many times discussed this choice that I would have to make. She advised me to follow my dream, no matter what. I promised her. So, as painful as the choice was to make, I left my entire family for over fifteen years to pursue my equestrian career.

part two

MORVEN PARK

THE TEST

I WAS TOO EXCITED TO SLEEP THE NIGHT BEFORE THE admittance test and woke up feeling scared and apprehensive. I never test well. If you asked me my name and told me it was a test, I'd hesitate. And this was the biggest, most important test I'd ever taken, the test for admittance to Westmoreland Davis International Equestrian Institute at Morven Park.

It was a two-hour drive from my home, and I arrived early so I could look around and familiarize myself with the grounds. The school was nestled in the rolling hills of western Leesburg, Virginia, in the heart of Virginia's Hunt Country, down a mile-long driveway lined with cypress trees. In the first half of the twentieth century, the Morven Park Mansion had been the home of Governor Westmoreland Davis, Virginia's reform governor. History abounded. The old mansion was now the carriage museum. It was astonishing to see that one person could own an entire museum housing more than fifty ornate antique horse-drawn carriages. The Museum of Hounds and Hunting and the Carriage Museum were on display in the old Coach House. The slave quarters had long ago been demolished. You couldn't even tell we had ever been there.

There was a gigantic indoor arena and five outdoor arenas, each manicured to within an inch of its existence. Many barns were scattered throughout the property, and the Marion E. DuPont Equine Medical Center was housed on the premises. The place was huge, over fifteen hundred acres, far beyond my imagination, with dormitories for forty students, enough barns and stalls for more than a hundred horses, a steeple-chase course, a cross-country course, and bridle paths throughout.

I found my way to the office, waited for my name to be called, and was ushered into the office of the director, Colonel Darley, for a personal interview. After spending what seemed like forever reviewing my application in silence, he seemed quite puzzled and amused. He couldn't believe I was ready to make such a big commitment after riding only once a week for two years. He was clear that I would have to work very hard to build enough strength in my legs and recommended that I run at least three miles every day until school started. I remember seeing a curious glint in his eye.

I was dismissed and assigned a working student, Jennifer, to help me locate the horse and tack I was to use and to assist me with finding the tools I would need to complete the grooming process, as well as the saddle and bridle. Thank God! There were three working barns and about forty school horses, and without Jennifer I would have spent the rest of the day just trying to find everything.

Jennifer introduced me to Jazz, a big chestnut mare that Colonel Darley had assigned me. The test required the ability to walk, trot, canter, and jump a simple cross rail. I was scared shitless. I'd never seen this horse before and knew nothing about her likes and dislikes. She looked like she was thinking the same thing about me. With Jennifer's help, the grooming and tacking up process went quickly and quite well. I did at least establish that I knew how to properly groom and tack up a horse. Louie would have been proud. After Jennifer helped me mount and adjust my stirrups, she casually mentioned that she had "never seen Jazz ridden off the lunge line before, and oh yeah, have a good ride." At the time I did not understand the significance.

After completing the walk and the trot parts of the exam, Colonel Darley asked me to remove my stirrups and canter a circle in front of where he was standing. It was dangerous for me to canter at all, not to mention without stirrups. I had only cantered twice before, and one of those times had been by accident.

Louie had told me repeatedly in my weekly lessons that my canter wasn't ready yet. She had been searching for a good, solid school horse with a well-balanced canter. We actually didn't have such a horse at the barn in Great Falls. We knew I was at a disadvantage here, but felt we could rectify the situation before school started, if by some miracle I got in. Of course, neither of us thought I'd get in, certainly not on the first try. We thought of this as a practice run. Anyway, Louie and I both knew that I hadn't saved enough money yet.

Ready or not, there I sat on Jazz, ready to show my stuff. I was scared and nervous and I used my leg with too much force. The sensitive mare took off as if she were in a race. She was accustomed to being cantered only in a circle on the lunge line (a 20-foot rope held by an instructor), and being untethered both surprised and excited her. Aha, now I understood what Jenifer had said.

Jazz took off at breakneck speed, around and around the arena. Within a minute, I was up on her neck, flailing about and hanging onto her mane for dear life. I was even too scared to scream. After what seemed like an eternity, Colonel Darley said very sarcastically, "There's no one up there but you, 'young' lady. If you want to come to a halt, you'd better listen to me and do exactly as I say." Perhaps it was his audacity to call me "young" lady that broke through my fear and got my attention, but I was astonishingly able to follow his instructions.

"Talk to her. Say whoa, whoa — and as she slows, get yourself up and back off her neck, and get your buttocks back in the saddle." As she slowed, I somehow managed to do what he said. "Now regain your reins. Pull back very slowly and gently, or you'll frighten her again."

I'm thinking, *Did he not see what just happened to me? And he's talking about me frightening her! Is he nuts?*

He came down from the stands into the arena, spread out both arms, and stepped in front of her. "Now come here, girl," he said. "Come here and quiet down." The mare stopped very courteously. He praised her profusely for being such a wonderful, obedient, gentle girl, and gave her a sugar cube from his pocket.

I dismounted, shaking like a leaf, my knees wobbling. Laughing and shaking his head, he said, "I think we'd better let you in here or you'll be dead before long."

I'm thinking *OMG. Things had suddenly changed completely. I was admitted because I DID NOT pass the test. What? Could this really happen? Was this some kind of joke they played on Black people?* When I called Louie to give her the news, she was astonished and immediately started planning a party for me at the barn.

Now my family would know that I had always intended to do this, that I had kept it a secret all these years. They thought I was going back to Virginia Beach to keep the old homestead. Instead, I was going away to a riding school for a year. I feared their reaction, as it turned out needlessly. My siblings were happy that I was pursuing my dream, and my sons seemed genuinely proud of me. So off I went to Morven Park.

Many years later I learned that Colonel Darley had already been fired when he gave me that test. The trick he played on me with Jazz, asking me to canter a circle on a lunge horse OFF the lunge line, was simply for his amusement. Not only was the game with Jazz a joke, but I was intended as a joke too. I, in fact, was intended as a joke on the new director who would be assuming his responsibilities in the fall just when I would be entering. Colonel Darley meant to make the new director's work impossible. Were it not for this "joke," I would never have been admitted to Morven Park. My grandma would have said, "God works in mysterious ways."

DEVELOPING THE SEAT

In the fall of 1984, I arrived at Morven Park for the first semester, breathless with excitement. I was over the top happy. I had waited for this all my life. I was also very scared, very, very scared. I don't remember if I was more scared of the horses or the people. My indigenous self told me to trust no one. The four-legged ones—horses—were big and had way more experience than I did, which made them intimidating to me. The two-legged ones were so rich and privileged they were culturally and ethnically foreign to me. There were to be forty students in the class and, as usual in my life, everywhere I'd ever studied or worked since I'd left home, I was the only Black person. This wasn't particularly interesting one way or the other to most of the other students, it seemed to me. However, the fact that I'd never owned a horse, driven a horse trailer, or even given a horse a bath, and could not canter a horse or jump a fence meant that I was most certainly not one of them—an equestrian.

On the question of race, or more particularly, my being a poor, old, Black woman in an elite equestrian school, I had nothing to say. My way of dealing with it was not to deal with it at all. I simply ignored the race question and any discussion of the matter. Pretty soon it became evident that you couldn't get to me that way, besides, I was at least twenty years their senior, the age of their parents. These people were kids to me, and I treated them as such. My lack of reaction and response to issues concerning race soon grew tiring for them and they let it go. I would have spoken up if I felt I needed to.

I arrived with a pair of secondhand rubber boots and no saddle, so I was definitely a curiosity to all. After all, this was Morven Park in Leesburg, Virginia, in 1984, a very prestigious institution catering to candidates for the US Equestrian Team (USET). Several members of the Board of Directors were also Directors of the USET. One of the directors was himself an Olympian. Some students arrived with their horses and trailers. Others had their horses shipped in by commercial horse transport.

The first few days were a whirlwind of activity—getting room and class assignments; meeting and getting acquainted with roommates; learning my way around the town and the campus, three twenty-four-stall barns, the horses, the paddocks; and getting to know the staff.

It was as if I were on another planet. I was entirely captivated and ceased calling home or visiting my husband. The boys were now both in the military. Family heard from me very sparingly. We were up early every day in order to be in the barn by 6 am. The routine was to first throw hay. Each horse was given a particular type of hay, timothy, alfalfa, orchard grass, and a specific number of flakes/slices. As the horses were munching on their hay, other students were washing out and filling their water buckets with fresh water, two buckets per stall. Fellow students filled the feed cart with oats, pellets, and sweet feed. As the feed cart was pushed slowly down the center aisle, students measured out each horse's portion according to the chart attached to each stall door. A mistake could prove deadly. Either too much, or the wrong kind of feed or hay, and you could cause the horse to colic, a gastrointestinal condition usually requiring surgery, and often fatal.

As the horses finished eating their hay and grain, each was fitted with a halter and taken to a turnout paddock to graze and relax in the cool morning air, especially those horses scheduled for the first ride of the morning at nine o'clock. We were to ensure that these horses in particular were turned out before having to go to work. They were calmer and more mellow if they had the chance to stretch and unwind a bit before being saddled and put to work—just like people.

Once the horses on the turnout schedule were outside, we mucked out their empty stalls (usually two or three stalls per day per person), sprinkled lime to disinfect and kill any urine smell, and put in lots of fluffy new wood shavings. You could actually see through the flakes. Often the new bedding would be so fresh and smell so good we'd lie down in it ourselves for a few minutes. That was certainly the first thing the horse would do when you put him back in his clean stall, lie down and roll from side to side. Once the aisle was swept and the tools put away, we could go to breakfast.

There were three large barns, each with twenty-four stalls, so this scene was repeated in each barn until everyone eventually showed up in the cafeteria for breakfast. If you had a good barn crew and everybody worked together, you could be finished in an hour. If you had slackers, you would get no breakfast, and if you were scheduled for the first lesson, you'd have insufficient time to change into your boots and britches and groom your horse properly. This would result in your late arrival to class and would mean embarrassing questions when you entered the ride late. If done repeatedly, this would have a negative effect on your grades and in extreme cases was cause for dismissal.

At the age of forty-two, I was even older than the school's directors and all the other staff. Finding a roommate for me became quite a challenge. The rooms were double occupancy with one bathroom for every two rooms. Which meant I was sharing space with three mostly naked, alcohol drinking, marijuana smoking, white girls. I thoroughly enjoyed all their pleasures, but I was much older and had to go to sleep at night.

All but one of the other forty students were between sixteen and twenty-one years old. Marie was twenty-seven, and after much ado, it was decided to board the two of us together in one of the staff residences that was not being used. Marie was from New York, the ethnic and racial melting pot of the world. Black people had been part of her landscape in New York, and she would be less likely to complain about sharing living quarters with a Black person. There had been some complaints when I was living in the dorm. The residence was a doublewide trailer with three bedrooms, a kitchen, living room and bathroom. Unlike the other students, we could keep food in our residence, and we could cook our own meals. We became instantly popular because both of us were old enough to drive and to keep beer and wine in our wonderfully private refrigerator.

Each student was scheduled for a one-hour mounted group lesson six days a week. Riders were grouped by skill level, which meant I was a group of one and therefore got a private lesson six days a week. Riders were also assigned their horses each day. The new ride list was posted in the cafeteria by seven am each morning. You'd get your breakfast tray and join your barn mates at the table to discuss the ride list. There was always lively discussion concerning why each person was assigned to that particular horse. The breeding, gymnastic capabilities, characteristics and temperament of each horse, as well as the skills and capabilities of each rider, would be debated by all. I was quite a bit short on both, but I learned a lot at the breakfast table.

After a few days of trying to keep up in the daily private lessons, the instructors all agreed and it was decided that I would benefit more from private lunge lessons. Lunge lessons do not require the rider to hold the reins. The instructor stands in the center of a circle made by a horse kept on the end of a twenty-foot rope, and you develop your seat, learning not to bounce in the saddle. To sit the trot on an active horse requires that you completely relax your pelvic muscles. It requires surrender. Your movement must "follow" the movement of the horse's back.

I began to show some progress immediately, but my body thought I had lost my mind. Places and things I didn't even know I had started to hurt. My whole body hurt. My seat bones were raw and bloody. It was such a mess "down there" even moleskin wouldn't adhere. There was nothing but tissue and bone to adhere to, no skin left. The insides of my thighs were rubbed raw, and my muscles were sore in a way I'd never experienced before. Everything hurt, including my dignity. After about eight weeks, I started to toughen up and become more resilient. I began to understand what the instructors were talking about, even if I still couldn't do it "correctly."

I learned that "correctly" was in the eye of the beholder and relative to instructor, breed of horse, and type of sport. I was in private lessons on the lunge line for almost three months before I progressed enough to be allowed back into the group mounted classes. Though still assigned to the most novice group, there was a change in the way I was received when I returned to the group lessons. There was no more snickering or finger pointing. In fact, it seemed that my difficulty and hardship had earned their respect. I hadn't run home crying as they had expected, and as some hoped. I was meeting the physical challenge as well as they were, even though I was twenty years older than anybody else on the property.

I was also not a quitter, and I was not going home. Unfortunately, I didn't have enough money to pay for the first full-year's tuition, $15,000. I had the $5,000 that my husband's mother had left me after I told her about the vision I had as a child, "The Right Hand of God." She had believed in my dream. In addition, I had scrimped and saved every penny I could. But I was not expecting to return after Christmas break because I didn't have the money for the second semester. I asked for a meeting with one of the directors, Todd Collins, so that I could explain why I was leaving.

Todd and I had developed a camaraderie early on. I had been assigned to muck-out, groom, and personally care for his two horses—the big gray 17.3 hands gelding, Brian; and Justin, the 16.1 hands mare. We both knew he had done this so he could keep a close eye on me and the quality of my work. One afternoon, as part of my working student responsibility, he sent me to the airport to pick up his parents. During this errand, I learned I was even older than his mother. After that, he took me under his wing.

After listening to why I would not be returning for the second semester, Todd briefly excused himself from the room. He returned with the co-director, Paul Lyons. Together they explained there was a position available in A Barn for a part-time working student. The school had been having a difficult time filling that position, and they asked if I would be interested in doing the job in return for my tuition, room and board for the remainder of the school year. I was speechless.

I ignored the tears that were rolling down my cheeks because I couldn't stop them. I steadied my voice and said very emphatically, "YES, I would be very, very pleased to accept the position."

There was just one more problem. I had gone away to school with my husband's blessing and encouragement, but since I had only enough money for half the year, he'd been expecting me to come home for good after Christmas. He was happy for me when I told him that I would be able to complete the full first year of the program, but quite apprehensive about how this would affect him and our marriage. My week at home was a bit tense, and I was glad when it was time to go back to school. I could tell he wanted me to come home, and I knew that I would not be coming home any time soon. We had discussed divorce, and I was ready to make it official.

A barn was where all the horses recuperating from injuries or surgery were stabled. I worked directly under the supervision of the barn manager, Simon, and became a kind of nurse's aide for horses. It was fascinating, tedious, and potentially dangerous work. I worked very hard and learned an enormous amount about caring for the injuries and ailments of equines, especially how their temperaments change during times of discomfort or stress. This experience served me well for the next twenty years.

My first call to help Simon came in the middle of the night. We were called to help with a birthing. The beautiful black mare was dying. She was stumbling about, falling into the sides of the arena, and then thrashing about wildly in the sand footing of the show ring. She appeared drunk, stumbling and falling and trying to get up and having it all happen again and again. I cried as though she were my child. Her foal was already on its way to the equine medical center for an autopsy. We all cried. We all hurt for her, and after Simon's injection, we mourned her loss. She was so beautiful. She had been donated to the school only six weeks before. She had been badly neglected, but in the few weeks we'd known her, she'd improved greatly, gaining over forty pounds. She was not a young mare, but she was magnificent to behold.

The next night I watched as Simon and two stable hands assisted Silver, a magnificent white stallion, as he mated with a boarder's mare. She was prepared and winking away. He was anxious until the moment of contact and then became very gentle. She then became very submissive, allowing him entry. They both appeared to relax and just stand for a moment, and then he expended. When he released her, she became triumphant, with a new air about her. She trotted away showing her best extended gait, tail waving in the wind proudly.

There were even more immediate benefits to accepting the job as a working student: I had Todd's personal attention and conversed with him daily about his two horses that I was taking care of. I received private lessons from him on how to properly lunge, a marketable skill. I was responsible for grooming, tacking up, and lunging the new donation horses under his supervision. I received private lunge lessons at least two to four times a week as part of training for the newly donated horses. Everybody got off my back; word got around that "Todd had some special interest in the 'ol' lady,' so make sure he doesn't catch wind of any pranks or insults intended for her." I had somehow acquired a nickname that I found quite offensive, The Old Three B's, the Old Black Barn Bitch. After accepting the job of working student, I never heard those words again. In fact, I almost immediately became everybody's new best friend—many falsely—and private counsel.

Being everybody's best friend ultimately grew into a problem, and I had to set up a 10 pm curfew at the residence so that I could get to bed at night.

SALLY SWIFT

IN OCTOBER OF 1984, A WORLD-FAMOUS RIDING TEACHER, Sally Swift, author of the number one bestselling riding book, *Centered Riding*, presented a three-day clinic at Morven Park. She was receiving worldwide recognition for helping riders with issues of balance and posture through better communication with the horse. I didn't want to participate because I feared embarrassing myself with a poor performance. Todd insisted that I ride, even awarding me a grant for the $650, the cost of the three-day clinic.

When I left the barn heading for the arena to join the others, I immediately became aware of a very unfamiliar sound. There were vast amounts of open space surrounding the arena, which sat on a knoll overlooking the property. As far as the eye could see lay the mountains of western Loudoun county. It was very foggy that morning, so I was walking up to the arena leading my horse by hand. As we approached. I heard the sound of many voices repeating "Ahhhhhhh," over and over, very slowly. The sound was reverberating from and through the metal building and into the rolling hills and open country. It sounded like a group of Buddhist Monks chanting in the fog. I was momentarily transported back to the vision I'd seen as a child, "The Right Hand of God." Even though I was running late I had to stop for a few seconds. I realized it shouldn't be possible to see a night vision in the morning fog.

The instructor, Sally Swift, had everyone mounted and walking around the arena without stirrups, with first one hand and then the other fully extended toward the sky while doing what she called the "whispered ah." I mounted and joined the exercise. After about three "whispered ahs," I began to notice a sense of stillness come into my awareness, a change of consciousness, space, and time. The horse began to notice something was changing and quieted as well. His stride became longer and smoother and just a bit slower in tempo but with increased energy. The horse raised and rounded his back, lowered his head arching his neck, and his mouth took up a light contact with the bit and my hands. This had never happened before. This was the elusive "horse on the bit" feeling that I'd been trying to achieve so unsuccessfully in my mounted lessons. I had spent so much of my time on the lunge line without reins in my hands that I had not developed the required sensitivity in my hands, and I had never been able to achieve this feeling before.

The other students, most of whom were my friends by now, were elated for me. Someone even went running to the office to tell Todd so he could witness this magical moment. Sure enough, he came running, and I was finally deemed a "rider" because in the dressage world, a rider knows how to put a horse on the bit. What I didn't explain was that, in fact, my horse had put himself on the bit because of the exercise that little old lady had us doing. I wanted to follow her anywhere. I had to find out how she knew what she knew.

The horse had always known that if I got out of his way, the most comfortable way for him to travel was with his back up and his head down. I was usually too tense and too stiff and too nervous to allow this to happen. The "whispered ah" had changed my breathing, and that allowed my seat to settle in the saddle, enabling the horse to relax and realize that I was giving myself to him. Now we had an exchange going on, so then he relaxed and the two of us became one energy, one movement, instead of me resisting and getting in his way.

I was so overwhelmed by this sudden success that when the lesson was over, I hung back until everyone else had left the arena, and Sally was gathering her personal belongings. I asked her if she'd like some help getting to her car. She immediately directed me to call her Sally. Very quietly, away from everyone else, I asked if there were any opportunities to do further work with her. Had she considered traveling with an apprentice? As she continued to gather her things, I began to assist her. She was in her seventies and the constant traveling to promote her book was beginning to wear on her physically.

Sally explained that, although she would love to have an apprentice and could certainly use the help, she had no horses, barn, or farm of her own. She taught as a freelance private instructor/clinician/contractor, so regrettably apprenticing with her just wasn't possible. I already knew that I was going to travel with her. I had dreamed it the night before. I had awakened suddenly with a fresh picture of "The Right Hand of God" being extended toward me. Call it whatever you like, I knew it was going to happen. For the remaining two days while Sally was teaching at Morven Park, I made myself indispensable and assisted her in every way possible. I schlepped and carried, in equestrian language I was *chef d'equipe*. Sally reminded me of my grandma.

What I found so impressive and intriguing about Sally's teaching was that she taught "how" to do something rather than "what" to do. Perhaps because of my advanced age, as well as having completely underestimated the physical challenge involved, I found her teaching method effective and a breath of fresh air. I needed to know "how" as well as "what." In classes I had received the same instructions as everyone else, but a forty-two-year-old body does not work like a twenty-year-old body. Sally's method helped me bridge the gap and fill in the blanks. Centered Riding addressed the physical challenges I was having, and my riding recognizably improved. After the clinic was over, I gave her my resume and asked her to keep me in mind should the opportunity for an apprenticeship ever arise.

THE SCHOLARSHIP

THE FIRST YEAR'S PROGRAM WAS DEVOTED TO TURNING OUT professional riders. The second year's curriculum focused on producing riding instructors. Two months before the end of the first year, a competition was held for scholarships for the second year. Since I had less experience than any student in the school, I had no intention of entering a competition. One afternoon as I was leaving the barn, Todd sought me out, calling out across the yard and approaching with a very serious look on his face. "Saundra, I don't see your application for the scholarship competition, and today is the deadline."

The question came as such a surprise that I was speechless for a moment, and then I said, "I don't feel I have enough experience to compete with these seasoned riders, and I have decided not to enter the competition."

He looked like he was thinking about it for a few seconds and then said, "You've forgotten one thing. I'm the one who will decide who gets the two scholarships, and I want your application on my desk before five o'clock." He excused me from my barn chores for the rest of the day, put the application in my hand, and sent me to the library.

The riding competition was being held on the weekend, two days away. Those students who had their own horses had been drilling them daily in preparation. Teachers were practicing with their favorite students. The horses were so clean and shiny they squeaked. I'd never competed before in my life, and most of the people I was going up against were veterans of the show ring, or at least their horses were. Some had even competed in Madison Square Garden in New York. The day of the competition, I was so scared that I went out behind the arena a couple of times to throw up. A stadium-jumping course with seven jumps had been set up, and each student was to pick his/her own course. It was not mandatory that competitors jump. We could choose to demonstrate our skills by riding only on the flat, putting their horses through lateral exercises and dressage movements.

Finally, it was my turn. Mind you, I had not practiced at all because I didn't think I'd be competing. Todd brought my horse to the gate. I was shocked. It was Justin, Todd's mare. He gave me a leg-up, adjusted my stirrups, and told me to get in jumping position. Because my seat was not developed well enough, I had not been allowed in jumping classes yet. That was the polite way of saying I couldn't ride well enough. So, this was all highly unusual.

He looked me straight in the eye and said, "Stay in jumping position, don't move, stay exactly as you are. You can close your eyes if you want to, just don't move." Before I could respond, he tapped the horse on the rump, and she glided off smoothly. Her canter was very smooth, with long, steady, slow strides. She headed immediately for the first jump. I closed my eyes, and my breath caught in my throat. It seemed like a split second, and I was walking out of the arena on a loose rein. It was over. I had finished the course. Everyone was standing, giving silent applause lest they spook the horses. Only Todd knew what I knew.

The horse knew the course and had even selected the order in which to take the jumps, had walked when and where we should be walking, trotted when and where we should have trotted, cantered when and where we should have cantered, and changed directions when and where the course dictated. There was simply no other explanation. The horse knew. I never spoke these words out loud, not even to Todd. It remained our unspoken secret.

Two months later the school's secretary came into the barn while we were doing evening chores, handing out envelopes to those students who had competed. When I received my envelope, I went out behind the barn to open it. I read only the first word, "CONGRATULATIONS," before I began to cry and rejoice. I thanked first God and second Todd, all at one time. I was awarded one of the two full scholarships for the Instructor Course, tuition, room and board paid in full, a small salary increase, and promotion to Assistant Barn Manager.

SECOND YEAR

I RETURNED TO MORVEN PARK IN THE FALL OF 1985 determined to demonstrate renewed vigor and commitment worthy of a scholarship recipient. After my morning chores were done, I took one lesson and taught one lesson, five days a week. I also taught twenty hours during the week at Great Falls Horse Center and on weekends at Rock Creek Park Horse Center in Washington, DC.

I was determined to work twice as hard as I did before to become a better rider. Working twice as hard meant more physical effort, which produced the tension I was trying to get rid of. The problem was more about me being scared than it was about my physical agility or ability. I wanted to show Todd that he had correctly placed his trust in someone who worked hard, but I was accurately described as a "timid rider." Horseback riding, no matter how well the theory is understood, must be experienced, felt, absorbed physically, must become muscle memory. My body just wasn't having it. I had improved immensely, but stamina and suppleness, flexibility and agility continued to allude me.

I still could not sit the trot and canter without my heart coming out of my chest, or so I'd thought. I would tense up just thinking about asking the horse to canter. Of course, the horse would feel me tense up and then so would he. We'd be back in fight or flight mode. Off to the races we'd go again. When you learn to canter and you're five or six years old, it doesn't occur to you to be scared. It's exhilarating. You're just having fun and you don't understand the danger. When you learn to canter at forty-two, it doesn't occur to you NOT to be scared. You could fall off and break your damn neck.

Even when your intellect tells you there's nothing to fear, your solar plexus and kinesthetic sense calls you a liar. It seemed the harder I tried, the stiffer I got.

In April of 1986, Sally Swift made her annual visit to Morven Park. This time she contacted me through the office to ask if I would be interested in trading the cost of the four-day clinic by assisting her while she was there. I was ecstatic. I had been praying for lessons with her, and to assist her would be an honor. The format and schedule was a repeat of the year before. Again, I was blown away. Her way of telling you "HOW" to do something, rather than just "WHAT" to do, was a godsend for me. She communicated on the physical level in a way no one else was ever able to.

She was quite surprised to see that though I had made definite improvements, I was still tense and physically uncomfortable when mounted. Sally told me about a riding instructor from Australia who was so impressed by her book that he traveled to the US and followed her from one clinic to the next for over three months. In fact, she said she got so used to him being there that she began to use him to assist her in her teaching. She remembered our conversation about an apprenticeship and asked if I was still interested. I think the world stopped for me at that moment. I couldn't believe my ears. Finally, she knew what I had known all along. After my tears of joy subsided, I agreed to meet her at the Denver airport in August to begin my apprenticeship. She had not had an apprentice before and wasn't quite sure what it meant, neither did I. But after some discussion about how we could or might define it, we decided to give it a go. All my expenses would be paid in full, and I would receive one riding lesson a day when we were teaching a clinic. Riders would also be encouraged to pick up private lessons with me. This would provide me with pocket money.

In this, her second visit to Morven Park, Sally introduced us to the Alexander Technique. She had very serious scoliosis and had been able to avoid back surgery by practicing this technique, which she called "use of self." The Alexander Technique is a way of freeing oneself from excess tension and muscle tone from within. It allows the body to function psychophysically in such a way that it enhances and promotes kinesthetic awareness. Sally was an avid proponent and practiced the tenants of this technique daily.

Much of Centered Riding was based on what she had learned from over fifty years of Alexander Lessons. By combining these two methodologies, Centered Riding and the Alexander Technique, I learned to give myself nonverbal directives when I felt fear approaching. During the four days of the clinic, suppleness, flexibility, and agility continued to elude me. Sally encouraged me to consider studying the Alexander Technique and offered to make some calls on my behalf. She was a frequent guest speaker and clinician at the Alexander Foundation in Philadelphia.

During my old modeling days back in Boston with Bill Riley, I had been taught to walk leaning my upper body back, behind the vertical. It was so well-ingrained a habit that I could not feel myself doing it. Unfortunately, I also sat this way on a horse. When I thought I was sitting or standing upright/vertical, I was not. This caused discomfort for both me and the horse when trotting. The problem had been frequently addressed in my mounted lessons. Sally had exhausted every other means, and now she was insistent that the Alexander Technique would hold the key for me.

I still had to complete my second year at Morven Park, but I got permission to do my required teaching off-campus even though students weren't allowed to leave the school grounds. I had been teaching at both Great Falls Horse Center in Virginia and Rock Creek Park Horse Center in Washington, DC, for some time. I needed to buy new boots and britches if I was going to travel with Sally.

As I began to include Centered Riding Principles and Alexander Directives in my teaching, I began to notice improvements among my riders: a newfound suppleness in their hip joints, an increase in their connection with the horse, more receptivity in the seat, and more sensitivity in the hands. As their seat developed security, their hands developed independence. They were no longer using the reins or the horse's mouth for support and balance. The riders in my classes began to be more comfortable and more effective. Several riders began to ask if they could switch teachers and ride in my classes. A few of the instructors joined my regular group classes so they could see what all the fuss was about. A few of them even incorporated the Centered Riding terminology into their teaching vocabulary.

I also developed a new ritual, doing Tai Chi in the middle of the open barn door, facing east, just as the sun was coming up. I did the Form before starting my barn chores every day. It became my morning meditation. Tai Chi was part of the curriculum at the Alexander School, where Sally had enrolled me. It's impossible to do Tai Chi leaning back. You'd fall down if you tried to perform the kicks that way.

Though the primary goal of the second year was to teach us how to teach students, the secondary goal was to teach us how to properly school horses. Anyone interested in teaching horseback riding must of necessity be equally interested in training school horses. Dressage movements and techniques are used to train horses because they are time tested and proven. Dressage is the International System of Classical Training Practices. Horses performing dressage movements often look like they are dancing. It is the most sympathetic method of training. Many use methods that involve more severe equipment and less ethical tactics. Dressage says, "The means is more important than the end." Any of us planning to teach riding would have to know how to train any horse purchased or accepted as a donation in order for the horse to become an effective "schoolmaster."

SNAFFLES

SNAFFLES WAS A SCHOOLMASTER, A HORSE THAT TEACHES the rider, a babysitter of sorts. As the least experienced rider at the school, I most often was assigned one of the best, most forgiving, and experienced school horses. Snaffles was a Thoroughbred-Percheron cross, 17 hands, solid, with a broad chest and big body. A small tank. He was newly donated to the school by a wealthy foxhunter in Leesburg, Virginia. Snaffles had been the hunting horse of the donor's wife. At sixteen years old, he was considered too old to continue the rugged jumping and lengthy sustained work required in the hunt field. He had a reputation for saving his rider in many dangerous and perilous situations. Snaffles and I had arrived at the school at about the same time, and Todd was training us both.

Snaffles was a beautiful dark bay, almost black. When he was wet, he was black. He had a very shiny coat and large luminous, kind eyes. It only took a couple of days before he began to recognize me on sight and trotted proudly over to the paddock gate when he saw me approaching. His back was wide and just a little raised and very soft. Sitting on him was like straddling a very soft moving mound. If you were sitting the trot, that mound could grow very hard if you tensed up your pelvic muscles. Ouch! The saddle fit him comfortably, resting perfectly on his back. Even with the saddle in place, you could still feel the muscles rippling under his skin when he walked. He had a long stride, so the ripples were big ones.

He carried me for miles and miles on all the bridle paths and trails, and over the cross-country course at both a walk and a trot. I often wondered what he was thinking, if he was thinking. Of course, he was thinking. I could tell by his reaction to things that we passed as we walked. He liked to walk in the woods best of all, along the stream with the soft babbling noises. He definitely did not like walking along the side of the road. Neither did I. The dirt road that led from Route 7 to the school's entrance and went on beyond the mansion and carriage museum had very little traffic, but sometimes people would speed up and/or blow their horns and/or throw an empty beer bottle at you, just for fun—the locals pranking the rich kids.

The sounds of the traffic, and the dust storm that followed disturbed and frightened us both. Snaffles's back would become rigid, his stride would shorten and quicken, and his ears would turn around backward, facing me. I could feel the anxiety in his body, but it was a chicken and egg situation. I was never really sure which one of us started it. I was never sure whether it was my fear or his that would cause him to take off at breakneck speed. He didn't do this if I stayed calm and centered. I could feel it when he was ready to take off. So we usually stayed in the woods, in the quiet with nature where the only disturbance was the glint or glare of sunlight bouncing off the occasional abandoned tin can or bottle. Snaffles taught me trust. If I was losing my balance he would move his body weight to support the place where I was faltering to shore me up, to give me the extra support when and where I needed it. Now I truly knew that God's Grace rode with me and he was providing strength for my weakness. At the end of the second year, I gave a very small donation to the school and was allowed to take him home with me. Of course, that meant I had to have a home to take him to.

CHOICES

WITH GRADUATION APPROACHING, I STARTED TO GET letters and phone calls from my family. My sons and my friends were wondering about my total disappearance. I had been missing from everyone's life for almost two years. Yes, I was beginning to miss them all too, but I couldn't stop just yet. I still had my apprenticeship with Sally.

Covance and I were hanging in the balance. He simply couldn't hang. He was a cool, handsome, sexy, motorcycle riding, Chicago born and bred, ex-semiprofessional football player. I needed a farmer who knew how to build and put in fence posts. It was already too late for us. While I was away at school he had lost his job and had been unable to maintain the mortgage payments on our townhouse in DC. He was living in a rented room on 14th Street, in the worst part of town. The bank had foreclosed on the house, so we got no money, and everything we had was put into storage. When he lost my house on Capitol Hill, he lost both my respect and my trust. I asked for a divorce.

At this same time, my close friend, Irene, was gravely ill. She was a travel agent and before I left on my apprenticeship had fallen ill in Italy. She was rushed back to DC where she was hospitalized and diagnosed with cancer. She lingered for several months. She was well enough to attend my graduation, and we continued the celebration at her house in DC over the next weekend.

It was too late for surgery. Covance had been staying at her house overnight lately because she had been released from the hospital again and this time sent home to die. She had several tubes in her arms, and often they would set off beeps and sounds that he found very confusing. We both became concerned that one of us was going to turn off or disconnect something and kill her by mistake. I also felt guilty as hell because my best friend lay dying while I ran around with a little old lady teaching horseback riding, although Irene would have it no other way.

Finally, I was able to get everyone to agree that Irene would be safest in a hospice. I did make it home for her funeral, but I felt so guilty I was unable to interact with her family and our friends and soon went home. Irene and I had agreed that there was nothing I could do for her, and she knew what equestrian school meant to me. Somehow, I could never shake the feeling that I should have been there for her.

Because of all this emotional conflict, my riding was suffering. I felt blocked, closed off, as if a door had closed in my face. Being at Morven Park may have required that kind of isolation, but Morven Park was ending. The apprenticeship was just beginning. I realized that I must somehow get back to performing my family responsibilities. I had become the matriarch, and I must make myself available to my family and friends again. I had not attended one family function in over two years. My grandma was turning over in her grave, although Mama was rejoicing that I had followed my dream. I often felt responsible to everybody yet driven to continue on this path I had struggled so hard to be on. Three more months and the apprenticeship would be over, and I'd be back.

GRADUATION

Graduating from school, finding a place to live, taking Snaffles, beginning and continuing the apprenticeship, interviewing for a job at Thorncroft Equestrian Center in Pennsylvania, accepting the job, and moving to Springdale Farm—all occurred over a short four-month period. There was a whirlwind of activity, and I was trying to find my place everywhere. Which one was my priority, which one should I do first, or should I even do any? Which one provided the most financial security?

Graduating from Morven Park's Instructor's Program marked the greatest achievement of my life, at least I thought so then. I got up that day around 4 am so that I could muck out early and get to the cafeteria before it got crowded. Took a quick shower, picked the hair, did the barn chores, and I was in the cafeteria by 6 am. I had new and proper riding boots that did not hurt my feet, a first. I could even walk in them comfortably. The shine on their toes was a high gloss. I wore my first pair of white riding britches and a beautifully tailored black riding coat. I looked and felt elegant. Snaffles was groomed to perfection. My leather saddle and bridle were polished to a gleam. At that moment, you could not have told me I wasn't on top of the world. I was so proud of myself, my heart pounded with excitement.

Graduation from Morven Park was a very formal, prestigious affair. All the students' parents and siblings were there, children aplenty. The Grand Hall had been decorated beautifully. Long rows of folding tables were set in a large triangle with room to walk or dance in the middle. White linen tablecloths were decorated with gold horsehead napkin rings. Beautiful fresh floral arrangements and candelabras were placed every few feet.

Two hours later, Snaffles and I rode into the arena to the sound of soft classical music and the graduation prelude. I joined a line of thirty-two mounted riders and waited for my name to be called. When my name was called, every student in the line took off their hat and raised it in salute to me, a rare honor and one no other student received that day. The entire staff stood and silently applauded. Applause must be silent because the horses would spook if there were loud or unexpected noises in the enclosed arena.

As I trotted over to the podium with tears streaming down my face, Todd handed me my diploma, wearing the biggest grin I'd ever seen on his face. I don't think anyone else was close enough to us to see the tears of joy filling his eyes too. Graduation was the happiest day of my life. All the other students had their parents and siblings in attendance. I was filled with pride because my two adult sons, my husband, and my three best friends, Irene, Walter and his wife, Evelyn, were there for me, the first African American to graduate from Morven Park. In my heart, I knew only God could have made this possible.

After graduation in June of 1986, I needed to decide where I was going to live and where I would take Snaffles. I first tried to establish a riding center in Olney, Maryland— Shananda Equestrian Center —with two other students with whom I had graduated. This turned into a familiar situation where I did all the barn chores, and they did all the riding and teaching. Unacceptable.

Snaffles and I moved to Richmond—me to an apartment and Snaffles boarding at a barn where I was teaching. This continued for a few months until I found a small farm to rent in rural Kents Store, Virginia. Covance and I had decided to give it one more try, and he came with me.

Whenever I was away with Sally or freelance teaching overnight, Covance did a wonderful job taking care of Snaffles. I was doing lots of freelance teaching all over the country. While living in Richmond, I taught at local stables and developed quite a following. I was even teaching lessons at Tuckahoe Plantation. Plantation is synonymous with slavery in my world, so I was aware of where I was and what I was doing. So too were the spirits of the slaves whom I could feel and see watching me and rejoicing as they shimmered along the tree line. Finally, one of us up on top of the horse.

Springdale Farm

The "Trackless Trail" led many slaves to freedom

Tina, Me & Sam

Deon & Zigi

Vincent, Me & Deon

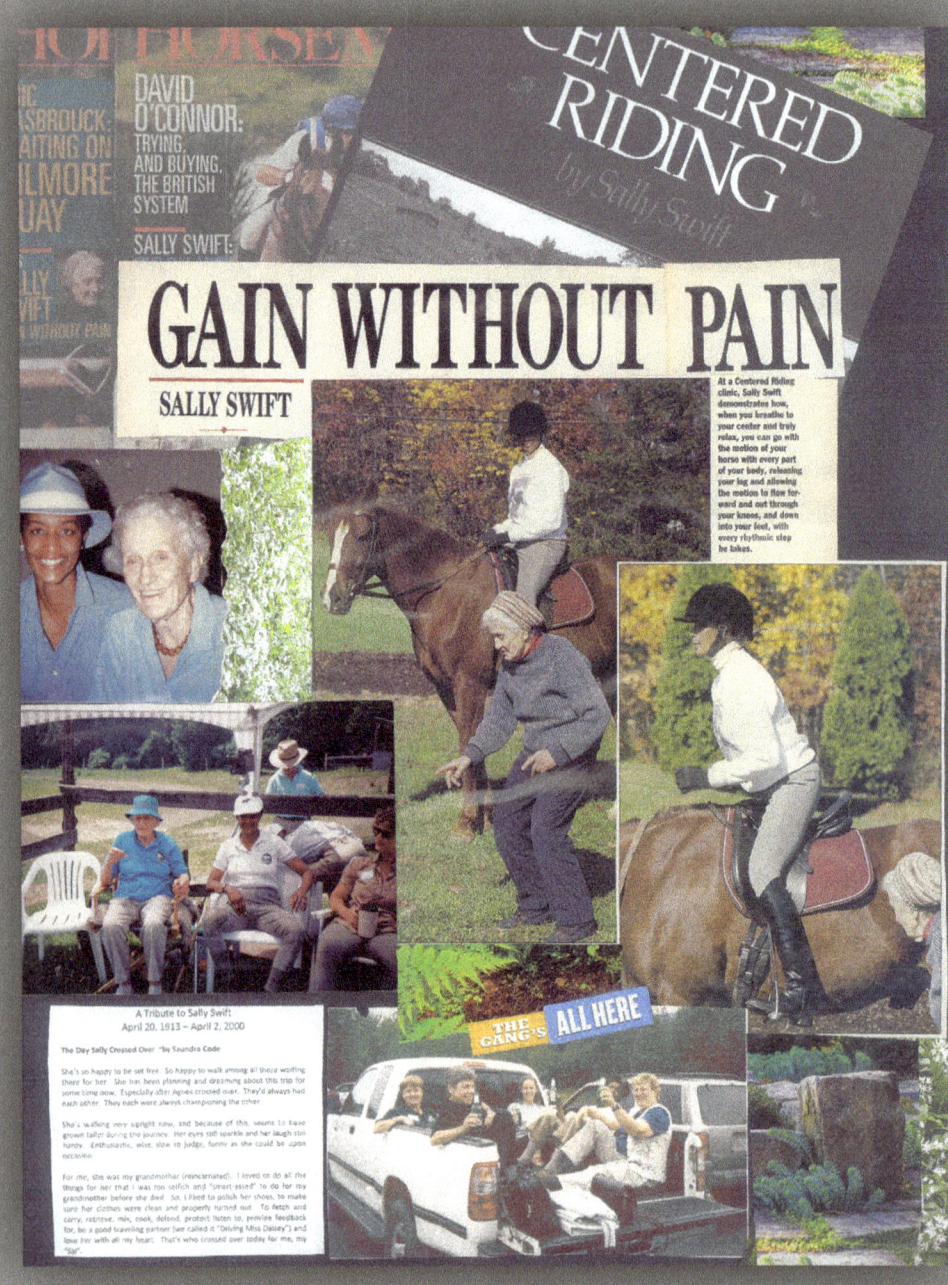

*I am forever grateful to the people who
bless my life, making these collages and my
life the beautiful works of art that they are.*

part three

TRAINING, TEACHING, & TOURING

PLANE, TRAIN, OR AUTOMOBILE?

THE APPRENTICESHIP

I MET SALLY IN DENVER IN AUGUST, 1986, TO BEGIN THE first of twenty-three Centered Riding Clinics I was to complete as her apprentice during a four-month period. I would assist her in the arena during mounted lessons and as needed "personally." Usually, an apprentice's responsibilities consist mainly of barn chores. She had no barn or horses and we agreed to define "personally" as time revealed the need. I did all the driving, and she was the navigator reading the map. This was all well before GPS. We'd often be so involved in conversation about my grandma, with whom she was fascinated, or about her sister, her only living family, that we'd pass our exit or forget a turn. But we always got there, regardless of whether we were on the west coast or in New England.

Sally was just about the same age my grandma would have been. I had been so mean and nasty to my grandmother, I think I was trying to make amends by going overboard with the personal care part of my job with Sally. I enjoyed finding ways to take care of Sally's personal needs as I would have cared for my grandma if I had not been such a little shit. As an atonement of sorts, I prepared Sally's meals, even learned how to cook that damn soft-boiled egg just right. I washed and ironed her clothes, polished her shoes, and in general, assumed the duties of a granddaughter, as well as those of an apprentice.

She could be quite comfortable wearing the same pair of pants for a week without suggestions to the contrary. In her old New England way, she and her sister had lived on a fishing boat with their father all summer long and no one took a bath. Her rationale was that we were constantly traveling, and the people attending the next clinic in another town wouldn't know that she wore those same pants at the last clinic. However, the fact that I knew drove me to wash them whenever we stayed where I could do laundry. I was much maligned for this excess by the apprentices who came after me. These were the duties of a proper *chef d'equipe* in the equestrian world, though they usually pertained to the care of the horse and his equipment.

The clinic format was always the same, lasting three or four days and usually over a weekend. Each clinic had four groups of four riders, with each lesson lasting an hour and a half—two groups in the morning and two groups in the afternoon. After the lessons were over, we'd cool the horses by walking them until they were no longer breathing hard, hosing them down to get rid of sweat and refresh them, putting them in their stalls, feeding them, and cleaning our tack. We'd then groom and dress ourselves for an evening of mostly horse talk. A glass of wine or champagne in one hand, and in those days, a cigarette in the other, along with caviar and such.

The days I spent as an apprentice were not without incident. There were the barns and owners who didn't have enough well-trained school horses for their paying customers and simply did not have an extra horse for Sally's apprentice—me. I could end up on a horse that hadn't been ridden in years or one that was completely unfit. One time, a horse borrowed from a neighbor had never been ridden before. He broke the reins and took off bucking when I tried to mount. Considering the "timid rider" I was known to be, I started to regret my privilege to ride in one mounted lesson a day. I began to see it as an unwelcome obligation. I found myself making excuses and really dreading what I'd be offered to ride at the next clinic location.

There was the owner who would not allow a Black person to sit at his table or sleep in his house. When the day's rides were over, I stayed back in the barn to help feed and water the horses, as any good apprentice would do. After washing up in the powder room and completing a quick inspection in the mirror, I entered the dining room, and all conversation stopped. Not a good sign. It took a few minutes for me to realize that there was no place setting for me, no empty seat. The man of the house sat at the head of the table and was facing me. He was mad as hell, eyes red, and mouth twitching. His wife, Lydia, sat at the other end of the table with her back to me, crying and shaking her head. They sat looking at each other, almost snarling. Sally stood up and said, "Saundra, you may sit here."

Then Lydia, the wife, clinic organizer, and hostess, stood up and said, "Sally, you may sit here." The daughter, Julie, stood up. She was a rider, and I had given her a private lesson earlier that day. We had shared great chemistry while doing barn chores together. She gave her seat to her mother. There were perhaps twelve or fourteen people at the table. Lydia was visibly shaken, embarrassed, and in tears. "Mister" left the table. We somehow got through the meal. I don't remember what we ate. After dinner, I was shipped across the road to a neighbor's house to spend the night. In addition to not being allowed to sit at his table or ride his daughter's horses, I also could not sleep under his roof. The neighbor was so embarrassed for Lydia and Julie that she overcompensated all evening, practically wanting to hand feed and bathe me. "Are you sure you won't have another piece of humble pie?"

Then there was the event at the home of the Fleischmann margarine heiress, an elegant setting with crystal chandeliers and velvet sofas, during which I heard drifting across the room on sound waves, "There's a Nigger in the wood pile, if you ask me."

Suddenly, yet in slow motion it seemed to me, every eye in the room turned toward me, waiting for my reaction. I didn't have one, not one that they could see anyway. I continued the conversation I had been having about which breed of horse I preferred.

Sally was not having it and stood up and asked her to apologize to me, which she did without hesitation. The room grew hushed, and I felt compelled to explain why I did not take umbrage at what was said.

"Inasmuch as I am not a Nigger, those words have no effect on me. So please continue your conversations and take no offense on my behalf." There was an immediate rush to the bar as cocktails were nervously and feverishly consumed. The mood and energy in the room had been compromised, and people started drifting out before dinner was even served. I wished I could have been one of them.

Surviving as Sally's apprentice meant living and socializing in an environment that was economically, culturally, and ethnically foreign. I did this willingly in order to acquire the exposure, skills, and experience necessary to confidently accept invitations to teach alone, particularly in England and Germany.

Our time together was precious. Sally and I genuinely enjoyed each other's company and traveling together for four months brought us very close. When possible, we'd sleep in the same room so that we could go over the agenda for the next day and get our lesson plan finalized. We usually requested a room with twin or two double beds, so I'd be handy if she had to get up during the night. She was well into her eighties and had neuropathy in her feet and legs. Even so, I still had a hard time keeping up with her.

Sally was insistent that I teach at least one group lesson a day. I grew confident teaching Centered Riding under her guidance and became quite an effective teacher. I was learning to combine the *what to do* I had been taught at Morven Park with the *how to do it* using Sally's Centered Riding principles, where students learned to use the body to inform the horse of their intentions.

Sally was continuing to insist that Alexander School was in my future. Surprisingly, I found my first Alexander Technique teacher, Frank Sheldon, in Charlottesville, Virginia, a mere fifteen miles from Cabell's Stable, the farm Covance and I rented just after I graduated from Morven Park. Frank was the director of an Alexander School there, and he was also interested in adapting the principles of the Alexander Technique to horseback riding. Frederick Alexander, the founder of the technique had been an equestrian, and Frank had several students who were riders. He and I were soon trading services. His hands-on lessons were introducing me to my kinesthetic awareness and proprioceptive sense. I'd never heard of either and was immediately fascinated. When Frank came out to the farm, he was learning to groom and tack up a horse. He would also spend about an hour mounted on the lunge line, learning how to walk, trot, and canter. We were both happy with this arrangement, but it was to be short lived.

The farm had a dilapidated six-stall barn, which we tried to spruce up to teach grooming and basic horse care. Covance was working two hours away at Dulles Airport. He often spent the night there in order to save on gas, and wear and tear on the truck. We had the land excavated, and we laid out an outdoor arena, though we were unable to finish it. I eventually had two boarders, but with no arena, they went on trail rides most of the time. We tried setting up cones in the grass to mark an arena, but the ground was so uneven the horses had a difficult time trying to do dressage movements with inadequate footing.

My older son, Deon, who lived in Washington, DC, would come out on the weekends to help put in fence posts by hand. He was twenty-five years old at that time. It was very hard, backbreaking work, but I couldn't afford mechanized equipment. We had no money. Vincent, my younger son, was in Jacksonville, Florida, with a new wife, Valerie, and a baby daughter, Antonia. He had also adopted Valerie's six-year-old daughter, Alexandria. He was doing quite well, worked for Mazda and decided to stay in Florida so that Valerie could be near her parents. I now had two granddaughters to get to know. Having lost Angel when she was five years old, I was thrilled. The more the merrier!

Sally continued to have apprentices after my tour with her was done. I think in total there were ten or twelve of us. In July of 1989, she and six or seven other graduate apprentices held our annual Centered Riding Gathering at Cabell's Stable in Kent Store, Virginia. The gathering was a time each year when we met to exchange teaching techniques and discuss the business plan and model for what had become a 301C incorporated business, Centered Riding, Inc. One of the participants at this gathering was Robin Brueckmann, who taught riding at Thorncroft Equestrian Center in Malvern, Pennsylvania. In addition to teaching horseback riding lessons to able-bodied people, Thorncroft was a therapeutic riding center for people with physical and emotional disabilities. Robin also kept her horse, David, at Thorncroft. They were quite an accomplished pair and competed frequently in US Dressage Federation events. She offered to give me lessons on David to help me with my canter work, if I could come to Thorncroft. I had always been interested in therapeutic riding and thought a trip to Thorncroft would be a wonderful opportunity to get a really great riding lesson and find out more about teaching in the therapeutic community.

In November, I accompanied Sally to the United States Equestrian Team headquarters in Gladstone, New Jersey. I couldn't believe it was me, little ol' Lorraine Ferebee, teaching horseback riding at a Centered Riding Clinic at the United States Equestrian Team headquarters. Just walking around in that rarified, beautifully immaculate barn with its cobblestone floor, polished-brass fixtures, and stained-glass windows, I smiled at God and thanked her over and over.

In December, it snowed about three feet, and the snow lay on the ground for over a week. Covance was stuck at the airport and couldn't get home. The airport was at least two hours away in good weather. The truck needed new tires, so he had ridden his motorcycle to Dulles and left the truck at home. Thank God he left the truck at home because the pipes under the house froze, and I had to go about a mile to my neighbors to fill up twenty-gallon garbage cans with water for the horses. I could just see their barn from mine, and it was downhill. I was scared. I might get down the hill, but because of the tires on the truck, I might not be able to get enough traction to get back up the hill. The horses had to have water, so I had to go down the hill.

Everyone in the county was calling the same few local plumbers for help with frozen pipes. It took three days before I could get someone out to the farm. His estimate to replace the damaged pipes was three to five thousand dollars. I contacted the owner (we had a rent-to-own lease) and gave him the bad news. He gave me his regrets and referred me to the section of my lease that stated all repairs and improvements to the property were the responsibility of the tenant—me.

THORNCROFT EQUESTRIAN CENTER

I HAD BEEN TALKING TO ROBIN BRUECKMANN AT THORNCROFT regularly after taking lessons with her on her horse, David. When she learned about my predicament with the frozen pipes, she arranged for me to have a job interview with Saunders Dixon, the owner of Thorncroft. He and I had spoken previously, and he knew about my interest in learning to work therapeutically with riders. I was hired immediately to teach horseback riding to able-bodied people who just wanted to ride recreationally. Simultaneously, I began training to teach people with physical and emotional disabilities.

After the apprenticeship with Sally and the failed attempt at Cabell's Stable, it was quite a relief when I was offered the job at Thorncroft. The stable and indoor riding arena were very large, often with three or four lessons going on at once. There were several outdoor riding arenas and a cross-country course. Classes were even being taught in surrounding fields. It was a very busy place with six or seven instructors. The stable housed about thirty working school horses, all breeds and sizes, all with easygoing temperaments. The large staff was seasoned and easygoing, except for one lady who disliked me on sight. She saw an old Black woman who learned to teach riding by going to a school. How ridiculous! "The only real riding instructors are those who teach from personal experience." There was this very friendly lady, Dottie, who scheduled all the lessons. She and I decided we must have had the same grandmother because they had given us the same advice on just about everything. We continue to stay in touch.

I rented a room on the farm in the home of the owner's ex-wife while I looked for a place to live. Snaffles had come with me from Cabell's Stable to Thorncroft, his board negotiated as part of my salary. I had to move quickly, first things first. Covance really couldn't continue to live in the employee lounge at Dulles Airport. It had been several months now and so far no one had commented or complained. The house back in Kents Store was just too cold to continue to live there, and the barn was not fit for a horse in winter.

Thorncroft had a substantial stable and arena just off the Main Line in Malvern. It was nestled in a wooded area surrounded by large pastures and some hilly terrain. There were many mansions in the area, and they all had bridle paths. The county laws did not allow the property owners to close the bridle paths to mounted traffic. Therefore, you could ride for hours if you knew where the paths connected. Several of them crossed shallow streams, permitting horses to pause for a drink when desired. Most paths were covered in shade by a canopy of large trees intertwined above, perfect cover in a sudden shower.

Thorncroft had a large contract with Bryn Mawr Rehabilitation Hospital. The hospital transported patients, each accompanied by a physical therapist, three days a week. I was teaching the able-bodied students, but in addition to that, I was creating therapeutic physical exercises that could be done on a moving horse.

When a person sits on a walking horse, it moves the pelvis and hip joints in the same way they are moved when we walk. So horseback riding is a way for the pelvis and hip joint sockets to practice walking without weight bearing—great physical therapy for those learning to walk again after an accident or surgery. Working with a team of five people—a physical therapist; riding instructor; horse handler; and two side-walkers, each of whom walks on one side of the horse, bracing the rider at the thigh to ensure safety—therapeutic riding lessons were very challenging for me in the beginning. My job was to assist the physical therapist who was responsible for the rider. I was responsible for the horse and its leader. We both were in constant communication with the two side walkers.

Often on sunny days, we would take a rider/patient out into the woods for a trail ride or to pick flowers or catch butterflies. We did this just because it's something most people in wheelchairs don't get to do. I remember one rider, Mr. Diggerberger, who had been unable to speak for several years following the trauma of a tragic accident in which he had been paralyzed. As we rounded a bend in the path, there stood a pair of deer and the horse spooked. Mr. Diggerberger, who was a retired minister and had not talked for several years, said, "OH SHIT!" We all laughed and laughed. I had worked with him for over three years before this happened. I not only laughed, I cried too.

SPRINGDALE FARM

I COULD SAY, "WHAT LUCK," BUT I KNOW BETTER. ON MY break at Thorncroft, I looked through the local monthly horse newspaper for a place to rent. I saw one, and I applied to rent the house on a farm owned for over a hundred years by the same Quaker family, the Mendenhalls. They boarded and trained event horses. They wanted to rent their spring house, which was once a station on the Underground Railroad used by Harriett Tubman, although I didn't know this at the time. I thought I'd died and gone to heaven. I wanted it so badly that I conjured up images of that arm in the sky, "The Right Hand of God," and I asked for intercession. So I don't think it was luck.

Springdale Farm was located eighteen miles from Thorncroft Equestrian Center, a thirty-minute drive. As I turned off the old country road, Springdale Road, onto the long, rutted driveway of Springdale Farm, there were horses grazing peacefully on both sides of the driveway. Following directions from Pat Mendenhall, owner of the property and barn manager, I followed the driveway past the main house with its fourteen rooms, three floors and an attic. The four pillars that held up the porch roof were each larger around than me. Several horse trailers, tractors, and lots of farm equipment lined the parking lot to the left of the house. The big old barn, three stories tall and well over one hundred years old, looked like it would fall down at any minute. If I were Little Red Riding Hood, I sure wouldn't hide out in there. The ground floor held fourteen stalls for horses. I'd never seen a barn like this. It was a converted cow barn. The stalls were all about, hidden in little cubbyholes or crammed between pillars and support beams. They were not the standard size for horse stalls and were used only when the weather was too bad for the horses to be outside.

I continued to follow the driveway on down the hill as instructed. I passed the covered arena to the right. The sides were closed up to about five feet high. This prevented the snow and rain from blowing into the arena yet allowed the dust to escape when it was dry outside. After crossing a wooden bridge, I finally arrived at a little four-room spring house, so called because water from an underground spring ran directly behind and almost underneath the house. The spring provided a constant, soothing, restful babble. Pat Mendenhall was sitting on the steps to the porch when I arrived. The little house was ancient. The floorboards were ten and twelve feet wide, and the stairs to the second floor were so narrow and angular that you had to turn sideways and bend over to go up the stairs.

The ceiling in the larger bedroom on the second floor was exposed log beams. It was a false ceiling, and the beams had provided perfect cover when the house had been raided and searched for fugitive slaves. There were enough beams for five people to lie on, and several more people could lie on top of those five and escape the probing sword blade or long knife plunged up through the ceiling by the slave catchers. A bay window fronted by a cushiony, pillowed window seat, the first thing my eyes landed on, gave a full view of the huge grazing field outside the bedroom window. It became my favorite seat in the house and looked out over close to a hundred acres.

As Pat started to tell me about the history of the house, a strange quiet, comforting feeling swept over me. I could sense the spirits of the many who had been saved in this house over a century earlier. I had just joined them, another soul saved by this house. Pat said she had always wanted to rent the house to an African American. "It's only fitting," she said. I immediately felt welcomed. The basement was just a hole in the ground about 12 x 12 feet and maybe 6 feet tall. Upon closer inspection, I saw that it hid the entrance to a tunnel that led to the railroad tracks on the other side of the cross-country course directly in front of the house. The tunnel provided passage to the north and freedom. The farm was the preferred stopping/resting place for fugitive slaves who were sick or had been injured because of the proximity to a freight train that ran across the Mason-Dixon Line less than three miles away. The train couldn't actually stop because that would arouse suspicion, but it could slow down enough for slaves to jump on and off.

The Mendenhalls, who owned the two-hundred-acre farm and after whom the town was named, were well-known abolitionists. In the attic of their house, they still had the record books of the slaves who passed through the farm during their escape. They had deeded to the state the land where the railroad track was located. That way, if the authorities found out about the use of the train to transport fugitives to the north, they would only be able to confiscate the land on which the tracks were located and not the entire two-hundred-acre farm. Many Quakers involved in the Underground Railroad lost their entire homesteads helping runaway slaves. I moved in within two weeks.

It was January 1990 when Covance and I packed up everything at Cabell's Stable in Kents Store, Virginia, and moved to the spring house at Springdale Farm in Mendenhall, Pennsylvania. Covance was not adjusting well. He was unable to find a job in Pennsylvania and continued to work at Dulles Airport, commuting by motorcycle four hours each way. The ride was particularly hazardous in the winter with the ice and snow. He had also started to have epileptic seizures but was in denial and refused medical attention. Because of the seizures, I insisted that he stop riding the motorcycle to work and buy a small economy car.

The following year, coming home from Dulles, he had a seizure that resulted in a car accident. He drove his car underneath the rear of a tractor-trailer truck stopped at a red light. The car was totaled, and we were lucky that he wasn't beheaded. After that, living in the middle of nowhere with no car was just too much for the Chicago born-and-raised native. One day while I was at Thorncroft, he packed all his belongings and asked Frank Mendenhall to give him a ride to a storage facility in the nearby town of Kennett Square. I never saw or heard from him again. Several years later, I talked to one of his relatives who told me he had returned to Chicago and remarried his first wife. I was very happy for him.

I was so glad, so relieved, when he left. He had begun to insist on accompanying me when I traveled and freelanced throughout the mid-Atlantic states. Several times, I had found him teaching little mini-riding lessons on the sidelines. He was also beginning to give advice on riding and horse care. This could have been very dangerous. A horse can kill you if you don't know what you're doing, and he didn't. It was I who had graduated from an equestrian school, and that education and training was not transferable to another person.

Because he had such a beautiful physique (that's what had attracted me), all the horsewomen at these riding clinics couldn't stay away from him. I was afraid he was going to get somebody hurt. So I said to him, "I don't think it is a good idea for you to come with me anymore when I'm teaching." If I had left the next sentence out, he probably would not have left, but I followed with, "You need to find a job of your own and quit following me around trying to do mine." I am pretty sure it was this last sentence that resulted in him packing up and moving out. At that point, I really didn't care anymore. I was just glad that it was finally over. I got a divorce.

FAMILY

When I settled into Springdale Farm, my son Deon and his wife went their separate ways. I was never told why. He moved to Springdale Farm and lived with me for almost a year. He acquired a horse of his own and took good care of him. He also learned to ride well enough to have fun safely. He often went with me on my freelance trips to the western part of the state. He did all the driving and schlepping, as I had done with Sally.

After a few months, Deon met a young lady at work. They hit it off, and he moved in with her shortly thereafter. They enjoyed a very supportive, fun-loving relationship. I joined them on weekends for flea market shopping, which we all loved. She had been sickly when they met. Diabetes and past drug use had compromised her health. Without any warning, Deon came home from work one night to find her dead in their apartment. She died of liver failure, and Deon went into a deep depression.

He moved back to Springdale Farm with me to try to figure out his next move. About the same time, his son, my grandson Jerry, who had recently graduated from Job Corp, was looking for a place to make a new start. He joined us at Springdale Farm for a short time. Walking five miles to go anywhere was not for him, and he could not afford to buy a car. So Jerry went back home to Virginia Beach. A few months later Deon moved back too.

Vincent was still in Jacksonville with Valerie, Alexandra, and Antonia (Toni for short). I was looking forward to visiting them for Christmas. Vincent was working for Mazda and driving back and forth to Mendenhall as often as possible. Toni loved feeding carrots to the horses and ponies that kept sticking their heads over the fence whenever she went out into the yard at Springdale Farm. After being away for such a long period of time while I was in school and traveling, I couldn't get enough of my grandchildren.

THE ALEXANDER TECHNIQUE

As I continued to take mounted lessons from Robin at Thorncroft on her upper-level horse, David, the Alexander Technique (AT) lessons I had with Frank Sheldon back in Virginia started to come more and more into play. I discovered that when I gave myself mental directives while riding but took no physical action, my comfort level and the effectiveness of my communication with the horse improved. Something happened, which I did not understand at all—increased kinesthetic awareness, from which I reaped immense benefit. I needed to know more.

I found that the AT is a physical way of freeing oneself from excess tension and muscle tone from within. This allows the body to function psychophysically in such a way that it enhances and promotes kinesthetic awareness and proprioception. Kinesthesia is the ability to perceive or feel movement, the relationship of one limb to another and whether or not that configuration is changing. Proprioception is bodily sensation that is not tactile and not sensations of movement: pain, pleasure, hunger, sexual feelings, tingling, and emotions (fear, anger, joy). Some say tension is an expression of emotion; others say it is resistance to emotion.

Alexander teachers are taught to use their hands to bring this awareness to students, who can then recreate those feelings and movement patterns when mounted on a horse. In this way, I was able to use my AT hands-on practice in my therapeutic riding instruction.

Frank Sheldon, the AT teacher in Charlottesville with whom I had traded services, referred me to Martha and Bruce Fertman, directors of the Alexander Foundation in nearby Philadelphia. Sally also called the Fertman's on my behalf. I was quick to arrange an interview and met them both. They were excited about the opportunity to teach someone in the equestrian field, both in terms of skill set and new marketing exposure.

The tuition was way out of my league—$7,500 a semester. After several private lessons with each of them, they suggested a compromise. They had a nine-year-old daughter, Eva, who was horse crazy. Would it be possible for us to trade services? If I would give Eva one lesson a week, I could attend their four-year AT Teacher's Program. Okey-dokey! I'm in! God Again!

So for the next three years, on Fridays after work at Thorncroft, when AT school was in session, I had a routine. I would drive to Germantown in Philadelphia to pick up Eva. That required one hour of driving. We would then drive to either Springdale Farm or Thorncroft for her grooming and mounted lessons. That involved three more hours. Cooling down the horse and cleaning tack took another hour. Driving Eva back home to Philadelphia from either Springdale Farm or Thorncroft took an hour. Returning home from Germantown took another hour. It usually took, depending on traffic and time of day, seven or eight hours to complete the entire process. I usually got back to Springdale Farm around midnight.

After a couple of years, Eva was more like a family member than a riding student. When I was with her, I often couldn't help but think about my daughter, Angel, who had made her transition in 1968. Eva often came out to Springdale Farm on weekends and during the summer to ride her favorite pony, Firecracker. Our relationship changed over the years, with me attending her school functions as one of the family, attending bat mitzvah and breakfast after Yom Kippur. I watched Eva grow from a little girl to a young lady attending prom. After Angel's death and decades of trying to act as if I didn't feel the pain, Eva was a balm unto my soul.

My AT training had become indispensable to the use of my hands in therapeutic riding lessons. Many of the children and adults had twisted or malformed retracting muscles. Using the AT hands-on techniques, I was able to guide and facilitate movement and relieve excess muscle tension in limbs. This resulted in students experiencing increased mobility, being able to stand or use their arms to reach for a toy, things they could not do when not on a horse.

The more I studied and practiced in school, the more proficient I became at using my hands to increase kinesthetic awareness, providing support and relieving tension in students while they were mounted by explaining and demonstrating how the body's natural movements can complement, accommodate, enhance, and influence the movement of the horse.

ENGLAND

I MET TWO WONDERFUL ALEXANDER TECHNIQUE TEACHERS from Oxford, England; Elizabeth and Lucia Walker were mother and daughter. Elizabeth was well into her eighties but very fit, and her teaching was strong and clear. Lucia was talented in her own right. Her father had been a renowned AT teacher. I can't imagine what it must have been like to grow up with two parents who were both AT teachers. Her posture and movements were to be envied.

In 1996, I was invited to England for their summer Intensive Study Workshop. While there, they also arranged a riding lesson for me with Danny Pevsner, the well-known author of the much-used pamphlet, Horsemanship and the Alexander Technique. Elizabeth's son was a champion horseman, and she knew many people in the industry. I was invited to give a three-day clinic on Centered Riding while there, but it almost didn't happen. I was looking the wrong way when I stepped off the curb to cross the street and was almost hit by a car. I knew that cars drove on the left side of the road in England, or at least I had read about it, but it was all just too new for me to assimilate. You had better believe I didn't drive while I was there. One roundabout and you'd never see me again.

The Centered Riding Clinic was held at what was once a working stable in a castle. Zora Natanblut accompanied me. She was my friend, a fellow AT student, and a physical therapist who was volunteering to assist with therapeutic riding lessons at Thorncroft. The setting was beautiful, right on the Thames River, which I could see from my bedroom window in the castle. This was a real castle. Lorraine Ferebee was living in a real castle. The living quarters were elegant but rustic at the same time, a complete contradiction. Having the chairman of the British Horse Society attend the clinic as a spectator one day was a bit intimidating. He was quite nice, complimentary about the Centered Riding concepts, and sent his personal regards to Sally Swift, whom he had met a few years earlier. We took pictures together, and he presented me with a signed copy of his book, *Dressage*.

While in a bathroom stall one afternoon, I overheard some students talking about the "American" who was visiting the castle. They were planning to invite her out to dinner and were hoping she would accept their invitation. I was very curious about this "American." Actually, I was jealous and wanted to meet the "American" also. It would be a real treat to talk to someone from home, but I didn't want to insert myself into their evening. I thought about it for a few minutes and finally, emerging from my stall rather shyly, I asked if I could meet the "American" too. A hush fell over the room and everybody started to look at each other. Finally, one of them said, "My dear, you ARE the American." I thought it odd that the first time I ever heard myself referred to as an "American," I was in a foreign country. The reference was not African American, not Black, just American. WOW!

The lesson with Danny Pevsner was overrated. It was a good lesson, but one lesson out of context with a master only served to ensure that those things I did not already know remained a mystery. Any questions I may have had seemed inappropriate, too elementary to ask, though it was rewarding to know that I could hold my own in the saddle among the best. My ego enjoyed the lesson and the whole experience. However, it did not improve my canter seat, which was what I had been hoping for.

It was here that I was finally able to let go of my criticism of my canter seat. Danny Pevsner had no negative comment about my canter work. He told me what I usually tell my students, "Stop trying to canter the horse. He already knows how to canter. Your job is to not interfere with his balance when he changes gaits. Allow the horse to canter." The extent to which you are able to abandon yourself to the movement determines the extent of your success.

On Danny Pevsner's well-trained schoolhorse, I had the perfect canter seat. I finally realized that the canter of a particular horse was equal to his training and experience. If I could afford a fourth-level schoolmaster, a couple hundred thousand dollars, I'd have the kind of canter seat that I so admired on upper-level riders.

THORNCROFT AGAIN

MEANWHILE, BACK AT THE RANCH, SPRINGDALE FARM, I was divorced and could devote all my time to teaching and studying. I continued to freelance while also teaching riding lessons at Thorncroft and in the covered arena at Springdale Farm. Snaffles, who'd moved with me to Springdale Farm, was wonderful on the lunge line in all three gaits, walk, trot, and canter, and was my schoolmaster there. I was also still traveling to other farms and barns, mostly in the did-Atlantic states, teaching Centered Riding Instructor's Clinics and updates at least two weekends a month. Often those clients would schedule private AT and riding lessons. So between my salary at Thorncroft for twenty-five hours a week, two-day clinics on the weekends twice a month at $500 a day, and the private lessons at Springdale Farm on Snaffles for $60 an hour, I was finally making enough money to open a savings account.

By now Snaffles was nineteen years old. One evening I went out to the field to bring him inside for the night, and he didn't come running up to the gate to greet me. I entered the pasture looking for him and saw him on the ground slumped against a fallen tree log. His eyes were closed and upon further examination, he had no heartbeat. He was the only horse I had ever trusted at the canter. He gave me my canter. He wouldn't let me fall off. If I started to slip or slide, he would move his body laterally to catch and right me in the saddle. I was never to canter with abandon again. We had been together since Morven Park. He was a true friend, and I will always remember his generosity.

At Thorncroft, Robin had long ago taken me under her wing. She and Dottie had trained me to work with all students, able-bodied or disabled. Thorncroft had contracts with Bryn Mawr Rehabilitation Hospital to provide equestrian therapy for their patients. Most patients arrived in wheelchairs or with walkers. Working alongside the physical therapist who accompanied the patients from the hospital, with my ongoing AT training and Zora volunteering at my side, we used Centered Riding theory, imagery, and terminology to effect change. We were favorite helpers among the physical therapists, volunteers, and staff. Zora was even taking riding lessons from me at Thorncroft. She also had trouble with canter departs. I was good at helping someone improve their canter if they already knew how, but not so good at teaching how to free up your body at the moment of initiation so you don't interfere with the horse's balance as he begins the transition from trot. I was supposed to be able to maintain my own balance, but oftentimes fear of falling got in my way and I froze, just for a second, but I froze. Only on Snaffles did I canter without this moment, because he would catch me if I started to falter. What a Horse!

I loved my work at Thorncroft. It was what I had envisioned the result of graduating from riding school would be. I could hold my own in the arena with the other more experienced instructors. There were always several lessons going on at the same time in the arena, so scheduling was everything and Dottie had it covered. Thorncroft kept about thirty working school horses, all breeds and sizes, all with easygoing temperaments. The staff was large, mostly all part-time, professional competitors. Dottie knew which horses worked out best for which teachers and scheduled the lessons to accommodate the instructors, the horses, and the riders. Without her clever scheduling, things fell apart quickly.

Centered Riding was presented in a language that was considered too flowery or lightweight for many dressage enthusiasts. Many of the traditional riding teachers didn't think much of the theory or practice. Robin was also a senior Centered Riding instructor, and having her at my side and Dottie in my corner provided the support I needed to deal with any difficult situations I might have with more senior staff. Although, after following Sally all over the place during my apprenticeship, I wasn't easily intimidated.

FELKENKRAIS® SCHOOL

WHILE STILL TEACHING AT THORNCROFT AND IN MY second year of Alexander School, I was joined at the Alexander Foundation by Sally Haney, the second riding instructor to complete an apprenticeship with Sally Swift. We both began to notice that several of the senior AT teachers were also Feldenkrais® Practitioners. They had a different quality in their hands-on work. They were more aggressive, and there was more movement, actual physical manipulation, of extremities. The AT work was more subtle, internal, kinesthetic, working with proprioception. I became fascinated with combining the two techniques and enrolled in Feldenkrais® School in the fall of 1997. The school was located in Baltimore. Sally Haney would drive down to Pennsylvania from her home in Vermont, spend the night with me at Springdale Farm, and off to Baltimore we'd go the next morning.

Feldenkrais® School was also a four-year program. The first two years were experiential Awareness Through Movement (ATM) exercises. ATM "explores developmental movement sequences following verbal instructions from a teacher." As I began to add what I was learning in Feldenkrais® School to my teaching skills from Morven Park and the Alexander Technique, the physical therapists who were part of the therapeutic riding teams began to take notice. In fact, Sally Haney, Sally Swift, and I were invited to do a clinic on these three modalities for the physical therapists who were participating in the therapeutic riding program.

I enjoyed teaching the AT because you could see the result of your efforts right away. I also liked that it was subtle and required that the student participate and be coaxed to release from within. I did not like the Feldenkrais® hands-on work. When we practiced on each other in class, I found the work too aggressive for me personally, too physical, too strong. I was afraid I would injure someone. I just did not like being touched aggressively, too much AT influence probably.

I did like the Feldenkrais® ATM exercises that I began to use when teaching riding. Often when you are teaching riding, you are a great distance away from your student. The usual large arena size is 198 by 66 feet. Being able to give verbal directions in physical movement sequences during mounted instruction became quite a teaching tool. It facilitated the development of an unmounted college class for riders using ATM. So after my second year and Sally Haney's first year, we became senior citizen drop-outs, although I did receive my Feldenkrais® ATM Certificate in 1999 for my two-year effort.

I taught at Thorncroft for nine years. My greatest joy was coaching the quadrille at the largest dressage show in the United States—Dressage at Devon, in Devon, Pennsylvania. I felt honored to walk the centerline of the main dressage arena for our demonstration of horsemanship. Half the riders were disabled, and half were not. Some were proficient, even gifted riders, and some were not. All were respected, worked hard, and had fun. It was my job to make sure that happened, and I took my job seriously. We practiced every Saturday, and our eight-member drill team, "The Mainstreamers," was very popular among both the parents and spectators at Devon.

DELAWARE VALLEY COLLEGE

MY FREELANCE WORK BROUGHT ME TO THE ATTENTION OF Karen Glassman, director of the Equestrian Program at Delaware Valley College, in Doylestown, Pennsylvania. Some of her students had ridden in a Centered Riding Clinic with me in the local area. She was having some issues with her private horse and wanted me to come out to her farm. These lessons resulted in her inviting me to teach a clinic at Delaware Valley College. The clinic was well received, and I was asked to develop a semester-long syllabus. I combined the three disciplines I had been studying: Centered Riding, the Alexander Technique, and Feldenkrais® ATM.

Delaware Valley College was located a couple of hours from Springdale Farm and the commute took its toll. I could not face the two-to-three-hour commute on the Pennsylvania Turnpike twice a day, three days a week. With a heavy heart and three months behind in my rent at Springdale Farm, I moved into an apartment in Doylestown.

Initially the students at Delaware Valley College were taken aback when they learned there was an old Black lady who was teaching some weird stuff called Centered Riding. However, by the time the semester was over, there was a waiting list for my class for the next semester. The program director declared that no one could take her Dressage 101 class until they had ridden in my class. I wanted to shout to the heavens, to my grandma, about this. I could just hear her telling folks up there about her granddaughter teaching college in Pennsylvania. I'm sure she'd still leave out any reference to horses.

While at Delaware Valley College, I was contacted by a former student I had seen ride in a clinic in Maine about her horse, Palomar. Palomar was an expert at lunging riders at the canter, a real schoolmaster. I had asked her to let me know if he was ever for sale. She had received many offers for him, but he was off the track and his legs had been pin-fired. She did not want him to compete again. At eight years old, she thought Centered Riding would be good for him physically. She approved of the way he would be used at Delaware Valley College in my care. Allowing him to be ridden by one of my students was always a treat for the lucky student and meant I did not have to pay board. He was obviously a school horse. I agreed to teach a three-day clinic at her farm in exchange for the price of the horse. She would keep the proceeds from the clinic. It's hard to be a riding teacher if you don't have a horse. Problem solved. God Again! The best part about this transaction was that I knew the real history of the horse and knew he could be trusted as a schoolmaster.

From 1996 to 2003, I taught the semester-long class at Delaware Valley College, Horsemanship and the Alexander Technique. The class met twice a week for three hours. The unmounted class, listed in the school catalogue as Movement Education for Riders, met twice a week for one hour in the classroom trailer adjacent to the barn. The class was about half AT work and half Feldenkrais® ATM exercises. The AT work was done primarily in a sitting position, sometimes using a chair or sometimes sitting astride a wooden horse form in a saddle. The Feldenkrais® ATM work was done primarily lying on a floor mat being verbally guided through physical movements. This work increased suppleness, flexibility, mobility, coordination, range of motion, and it improved the balance of the rider. This, in turn, allowed the rider to improve communication with the horse.

GERMANY

IN 2000, BRUCE AND MARTHA FERTMAN, MY MENTORS FROM the Alexander Foundation and Eva's parents, were holding a month-long intensive study course in Germany. Germany is the home of dressage, as we knew it then, and many participants in the course were horseback riders. The Fertmans needed staff who could work with riders. Having watched Eva's growth and development as a rider, they had great trust in my skills. Thus, I was invited to accompany them, all expenses paid, and I could attend any of the classes I chose when I was not working. I was honored. God Again! Ain't She Good!

Being out of the country for four weeks was a little disorienting. It didn't get dark until after 9:30 pm. I couldn't find any books written in English. There was no American music or radio. I had cheese with wine for breakfast. I had to teach using an interpreter. I had to walk nearly two miles to not be seen from a window in order to sneak a cigarette. It was hard to be in such a restrictive environment for so long. I enjoyed the experience, but I was ready to go home, not just to America, but back to Virginia Beach.

I returned to Delaware Valley College where I was still teaching mounted lessons five days a week and managing the barn in the morning through feeds and chores. This made me a bit unpopular because, unlike the last barn manager, I insisted students show up on time and do the work. I was the only instructor in the Equestrian Program to fail a student. Four unexcused absences and you're out— straight and simple. Barn chores could all be completed in one hour, if everyone showed up on time and pitched in.

In 2003, after seven years at Delaware Valley College and

fifteen years living away from my family and culture, the need to go home became overwhelming. I had intended to go back to my family once the apprenticeship with Sally was over, but then the AT and Feldenkrais® School happened. Because of that, I kept getting invitations to teach that I couldn't refuse. I had been living the life, traveling all over the place, living in mansions and castles and on estates with hundreds of acres, provided with private quarters— sometimes even a house of my own. I was enjoying the work and the lifestyle. However, I realized I was living a lie. I was a pretender. I had everything at my disposal, the best of horses and accommodations, but I owned nothing. I was actually a homeless person.

part four

GOING HOME

VIRGINIA BEACH

THE SUMMER BEFORE I MOVED, I'D HAD A DREAM IN WHICH I saw myself as an old, old lady living in luxury in someone's grandiose mansion on a lovely farm with a beautiful barn full of the best horses ever; and they decided I was too old to do this kind of work anymore and fired me. Although this moving about was standard practice in the equestrian industry, I decided I needed to get the hell out of Dodge and find a place to settle down.

In July of 2003, at the age of sixty-five, I moved from Pennsylvania back to my hometown, Virginia Beach. It was wonderful just to smell the salty sea air again, to see familiar wildflowers blooming, and to hear birds singing familiar songs.

Since I did not actually have a home to return to (we had sold the homestead after Mom died), I stayed with my best friend, Tina, and her husband, Sam, for two weeks until I found a place. Tina and I had met when we were nine years old, and we are best friends even now. It's like a marriage, until death do us part.

On Sunday, July 7, 2003, I received the keys to a wonderful little three-bedroom townhouse with a tiny backyard. The rent was reasonable, and the backyard was just big enough to lay out a garden for morning meditation. I loved it. The rooms were small, but the living room had a fireplace, which made up for anything else that might not have been up to par.

I came home to Virginia to build a nest, to have a place to hibernate and meditate. It was the right decision, and I was happier than I could remember being since I was a little girl living at my grandma's house.

I found work teaching riding at a local stable that had the dirtiest barn and arena I'd ever seen. I still had Palomar with me, and again he was used as a schoolmaster. I would have been very embarrassed if anyone I knew in the equestrian industry saw me in this kind of environment. I was truly a snob by then, but I couldn't afford to pay board for Palomar. That and my need to eat kept me going back every day. Nights I worked at a nearby Barnes & Noble.

I also rejoined the church of my youth and experienced what it felt like to sing in a gospel choir again. I had missed this environment so much over the last fifteen years. I found myself going to church almost as much as my grandma had. I was singing and shouting all over the place. It felt so good to be there, to feel that soul-stirring, foot-stomping music of my childhood once more. I even went to prayer meetings during the day. I had clearly been starving for this renewal of spirit that could only be had in an old Southern Baptist Church. My baby brother, Joseph, was now a deacon in this church. I could feel my grandma's approval.

I had loved my life and career, but after so many years of being away from family and living in another culture, I wanted to be near my grandchildren more than anything else. I had never really gotten to know them. I had been away touring and teaching during their childhoods and most of the time neglected to even send birthday cards and Christmas presents. They were all in Virginia Beach now.

By this time, I had been away from family and living exclusively in the equestrian world for fifteen years, and I felt I could only last so long as an aging equestrian. My hip joints decried my situation. In August 2002, I had taught a four-day Centered Riding Clinic in Oregon. At the closing event on the last night, I saw "my vision" in the sky once again, "The Right Hand of God." That evening Spirit sang through me the hymn "Amazing Grace," and I knew I was saying goodbye to the equestrian life. The following lovely poem was written and read to me by one of the riders in the clinic. Just after that, I turned in my resignation at Delaware Valley College.

On Saundra

The black instructor spoke of retiring, of returning to her roots—to family, to her best friend from many lifetimes ago. She spoke of the need for a loving hug every day—not from her adoring white students but from immediate family sharing skin color, kin and culture. And when she spoke of her family and past, small nuances in her voice and inflection relaxed. The pretense of her erudition no longer guided her speech which now came with ease and humor and longing.

It was the final day of a four day clinic. She and her students were celebrating with wine and barbeque allowing the intensity of concentrated teaching and learning to melt in to the soft summer evening of chatter and eating and entertainment. One student brought a guitar and sang in a lilting and pretty country white girl kind of way. The black teacher, a teacher of breath and air, of feel and allow, helped the girl as she sang, find the source of her voice in the ground, helped her release it up and out into the night sky.

Jovial, half drunk, exhilarated by the sweet release, the other students begged for more, for the teacher herself to sing. Their voices overlapping, chattering, their attention diverted by the swaying and dancing of each other's bodies; the teacher sat waiting. She lowered her eyes. The pleas for more song resumed, and still she waited. their chattering never subsiding. Then, from the hubbub arose a sound, so soft, like the earth murmuring. So low began the sound, so deep and ancient as though rising from antiquity to fill the present with a startling beauty that hushed the white voices, stunned them into silence.

As the teacher's voice rose and descended and wrapped around them, her students realized her gift was not only of body sense and breath. She also gave them her yearning, which can be only sung. She gave them her need to leave them, her source, her self. She gave to them in spite of their differences. And only then did they realize how much they would miss her. When the voice stopped, the sound returned to earth, she, with typical humor and humility — in case someone might take the moment too seriously, said "I don't see myself as a singer, I just love to sing". Finally reminding her students that they must not worry themselves with being, only becoming. and of course breathing.

Judith Ogus
August 18, 2002

It was 1966 when I left Norfolk, Virginia, with Tony headed for Boston. It was 2003 when I returned, thirty-seven years later. I went immediately to the oceanfront to dip my feet in the waters of the Atlantic. It was a family ritual, a time for prayer and thanksgiving.

Dipping our feet in the ocean was symbolic of going home again. On the other side of the Atlantic Ocean was Africa.

I absolutely loved being back. The air smelled delicious, like the ocean. The clouds looked different too, different from anywhere I had been, lots of big cumulus clouds, big fluffy affairs. I went to Ocean View Beach near Deon's apartment, which he shared with his son Jerry. The morning surf was up, very volatile with remnants of Hurricane Isabel off the coast. There were no gulls, but lots of debris and seaweed, huge waves, and lots of white caps everywhere. There seemed to be nothing but endless blue and green, sky and sea, unable to tell which was which or where the two met. Deon was swimming within sight, and it was very, very windy. My umbrella took to the air and out to sea. Deon rescued it.

I was soon busy teaching horseback riding two days a week and shelving books at Barnes & Noble five evenings a week. Most of my riding students were beginners, both children and adults. The adult beginners were mostly empty nesters. My job was to first make sure they enjoyed the lesson and second to teach them how to ride. The people I worked with were good-natured and the job was low-key. The kids were fun, and I enjoyed teaching adults about kinesthetic awareness.

I was decorating my new townhouse and spending as much time in front of the fireplace as possible. My sons were well and doing fine, considering it had been a rough year for Deon. After his fiancée had passed away, he had moved back to Virginia Beach, but his three children and ex-wife did not welcome him back into their lives. I had planned to spend some long-awaited quality time with them. I couldn't wait to get to know my grandchildren, especially my granddaughter who everyone said looked like me. Little did I know she was not looking forward to getting to know me. With encouragement from her mother, she wanted nothing to do with either me or her father. I couldn't blame her; she didn't know my heart. Though we met several times during holidays, I regret we have not grown close.

JACKSONVILLE

IN JULY OF 2003, MY DAUGHTER-IN-LAW, VALERIE, AND granddaughter, Toni, came to visit me in Virginia Beach. I had enjoyed being with my granddaughter so much that I decided to move to Florida with the expectation that she would be interested in riding horses and spending time with me. I was so hungry to be included in their lives that I couldn't get enough. Both sons had married girls I had never met, girls they met when we lived in Boston and the boys spent the summers in Virginia Beach working to earn money to buy school clothes—Doyletown girls.

Vincent's second wife, Valerie, and their two girls were his new passion. She was from Jacksonville and wanted to raise the girls near her parents since I was traveling all the time. Nobody actually told me they would spend time with me if I moved to Florida, but I so longed to rebuild that feeling of family connection I had as a child that I made that assumption. I was wrong.

NEW YORK

Talking with Tina on the phone one day, the subject of people we wished we had not lost touch with came up. I mentioned Tony, the man I had headed to Boston with in 1966. She entered his name in a search engine and came up with an address in Boston that I recognized. I decided to write him at that address to see if he was still there or if anyone knew of his whereabouts. He called me a few days later to let me know that he was in New York. We made plans for me to visit, and we were married within ninety days on July 4, 2010. We were roommates and trusted friends. At his age, potency and interest had waned, so he was no longer chasing or running women. I was not willing to work as hard as would be required to awaken it. Anyway, too much belching, farting, and teeth grinding for my taste.

New York provided endless opportunities for exploration, and I made full use of them. A co-worker at Barnes & Noble told me that the city was recruiting applicants for the mounted park police. Naturally, I signed up, passed the mounted examination, completed the academy training, and got a chance to use all the skills I had learned in equestrian school, in my apprenticeship, and while teaching and touring. This was a chance to work with horses in the city. I had to!

I had often longed to once again experience the graceful, buoyant, full of volume feeling you get when you sit on a horse. To experience what it feels like to be mounted upon something as elegant and noble as a draft horse, listening for your commands, soft in the mouth, and light in the hand; his back up and moving in big gentle rolling movements, as though your hip joints were peddling a bicycle backward. But wait. How'd we get here? That's another story. I was talking about how I came to be sitting on a police horse in Central Park.

It had been seven years since I'd sat on a horse. The fog was thick that morning. I couldn't even see the tops of the Manhattan skyscrapers. I sat straddling Monte, the big black Percheron gelding I often rode on patrol. We were on the beautiful, tree-lined, immaculately manicured Central Park bridle path. My mind couldn't resist reminiscing about the long, winding road that led me to becoming an Auxiliary Mounted Park Enforcement Officer. It had taken me twenty-eight years to arrive at this day; that's when my training had begun. Yet, in another way, it had taken me sixty-five years, because that's how long it had been since I saw my first horse. So yes, sitting there mounted on a police horse in Central Park was most definitely a dream come true. WOW!

Monte didn't seem to share my thoughts. He dozed off and on, bored with the quiet, uneventful day. As a police horse, he'd had his share of active patrols with lots of noise and protesters or demonstrators throwing bottles at him and calling out derisive names. Once someone even spit in his face. I used my baton that day.

This day would be hot but with a nice breeze. The park goers were mostly Europeans on vacation with a few sunbathers on the Green. There were the usual dog walkers trying to escape the park's dog leash law. I felt privileged and honored to be in uniform and on Monte. I felt that everything else I had ever done with horses was to enable me to be here now. Silent tears of praise and thanksgiving went up every day I rode. I felt I had finally arrived. I had "made something of myself." This was certainly a long way from Doyletown.

It had been seven years since Tony and I married, and I moved to New York. It was certainly not what I expected it to be, but it worked, and I was happy. Fortunately, Barnes & Noble was only three blocks away from the apartment, and I went to work immediately for pocket money. God Again! We both got what we signed up for. He got a bookkeeper and a cook, plus financial assistance since I paid half the rent. I got a place to live that I liked and enjoyed.

Tony is a homebody and I'm the outdoorsy, exploring type. Having spent his most virile years dealing drugs, there had always been lots of women around begging to provide any sexual favors he could invent in exchange for unlimited cocaine. So he never learned about romance and giving pleasure to a woman. Therefore, romance was never a part of our arrangement. We never consummated our marriage. We decided to let sleeping dogs lie. I am grateful that he is a kind, good natured, and gentle man.

Tony's health had become a concern for me. Living in

Manhattan began to offer challenges. I started watching the old people entering and exiting the subway stations and trains with their walkers, canes, and wheelchairs. I decided I did not want to become one of them.

    The first time I moved to Jacksonville, it was all about my granddaughter. It didn't take long for me to learn how short sighted that was. This time was very different. I was moving because Tony had been diagnosed with dementia, and I was having difficulty taking care of him alone. My safety and well-being in Manhattan was jeopardized. Manhattan is probably the most expensive place one can live in America. Though I loved living there, we simply could not survive financially on two social security checks.

JACKSONVILLE AGAIN

My son Vincent had been living in an empty house in Jacksonville since his divorce in 1994. He and his brother, Deon, decided it was time for me to be with family again. I agreed, and Tony and I moved to Florida in July 2017.

From 1986 to 2015, twenty-nine years, I made my lifelong dream come true, working in a new, obscure profession where there is little paid employment for outsiders. Training and equipment are very expensive and access to adequate facilities is very limited, both geographically and financially. But I DID IT, I LIVED IT, I LOVED IT, AND I'D EVEN DO IT AGAIN IF I COULD. I feel my mom smiling.

We can live many lives during one lifetime. I have recreated myself every twenty years, so how many more lives can you live while yours lasts? Just do what's before you next, but never give up your dream. That's what I have learned by living my life my way. And my way is to repeat my favorite mantra whenever I'm not sure of what to do next. HIS will, HIS way.

ABOUT THE AUTHOR

Born Lorraine Sandra Ferebee and raised in Virginia Beach, Virginia, Lorraine graduated from Westmoreland-Davis International Equestrian Institute at Morven Park in Leesburg, Virginia, in 1986 and was soon certified by the American Riding Instructor Certification Program. After graduation she traveled throughout the US with Sally Swift, author of *Centered Riding*. Lorraine completed the four-year teacher training program at the Alexander Foundation in Philadelphia, becoming an Alexander Technique Teacher. She also completed a two-year study of Feldenkrais® Awareness Through Movement.

Saundra combined these three disciplines and created a unique semester-long syllabus and curriculum: Classical Riding and the Alexander Technique, which was published in *Dressage Today*, July 2001. She taught this class at Delaware Valley College in Doylestown, Pennsylvania, for several years while continuing to travel throughout the US and abroad, teaching three- and four-day Centered Riding clinics.

While living in New York City, Lorraine served as an Auxiliary Mounted Officer for the New York City Park Enforcement Patrol. She was also invited to join the Harlem Writers Guild. Along with her husband, this mother of three, grandmother of five, and great-grandmother of five currently resides in Jacksonville, Florida.

Lorraine's experiences and adventures proved to be fertile ground for this memoir. Her vision is to see this book produced as a film.

Shanti Arts

Nature · Art · Spirit

Please visit us online
to browse our entire book catalog,
including poetry collections and fiction,
books on travel, nature, healing, art,
photography, and more.

Also take a look at our highly regarded art
and literary journal, *Still Point Arts Quarterly*,
which may be downloaded for free.

www.shantiarts.com